Yes, Lord

"Yes, Lord. You know I love you."

Simon Peter circa 30 AD

By Boyd Hopkins

Yes, Lord

Library and Archives Canada Cataloguing in Publication
ISBN 978-0-9917023-2-9

Design by Myra Herman
Author and Cover Photos by Stuart Kasdorf
Cover Design by Shaun Salen
Printed in Canada by Globe Printers, Saskatoon, SK

Acknowledgements

Many thanks to those who have contributed to the writing of this book.

Thanks to Ed Strauss, Alison Uitti and Alice Berggren for editing the material in these pages, to Shaun Salen and Stuart Kasdorf for their cover design and photography, and to Myra Herman for the layout design. Thank you to my wife, Jacqueline Hopkins, for her support and encouragement along with the many others who encouraged me to put these devotionals into book form. Above all, I give thanks to my Lord Jesus Christ who calls us to the freedom we were created for. May He bless each of us as we engage His calling.

"I love Yes, Lord! Boyd's writing has the same attention-gripping style as his speaking. He cuts right to the heart of issues while bringing solid Bible teaching to the reader. Prepare to be challenged as you are invited to a deeper surrender to Jesus!"

Linda Kasdorf, BSW – RSW, School Counsellor

"In Yes, Lord, the reader is invited to participate in a very personal, spiritual journey. Boyd writes with the resolve of drawing people into a closer walk with Jesus Christ using the Word of God and enriching prayers. I encourage you to study and follow the directives thoroughly. Your spiritual life will have a profound transformation."

 Dr. Bruce Pringle, M.Ed., Ph.D.

"Boyd Hopkins writes with a humble authority about a lifestyle of prayer and Bible meditation. Truths of Scripture come alive under his wise and sometimes provocative style of engaging the reader."

Coralee Nelson, M.Ed.

"In Yes, Lord, you will find a place where a broken heart will find hope, a passionate soul will find direction, a questioning spirit will find safety, and a searching mind will find answers. Here is a place where the Living God speaks His message of hope and healing right in the middle of everyday life."

Pastor Brian Tysdal, Rock of Ages Church, Saskatoon, Canada

Welcome to *Yes, Lord*

Some time ago I sat down to write an online series of short daily devotions. The writing process soon morphed into a personal journey of discovery at a time when God was teaching me how to trust Him more deeply. Due to their increasing length and the fact that I sometimes got lost for hours at a time in what I was writing, my original plan to write one per day dropped away and they became the "Almost Daily Devotionals." I decided to put them together into book form. After reading through the material, my editor told me that there was enough flow to the writing that he felt many people would simply pick it up and read it in one sitting. It had become more than a simple devotional book and now needed to be renamed.

From the opening chapter on what it means to "repent and believe" to the closing chapter on Jesus' restoration of Peter, the theme is about surrender to Christ and dependence on His strength rather than on my own. It's about giving Him my "yes" in as many ways as I can. To that end, I have called this book *Yes, Lord*.

As *Yes, Lord* developed, I became convinced that I had to help you, the reader, take action on what you were reading, so I added prayer times to the end of each chapter. Each prayer time is intended to facilitate an encounter with the living God as you respond to the Holy Spirit's invitation to say "yes" to Him. The prayers are patterned after Jesus' call to repent and believe in Mark 1:15. My hope is that you will experience a deeper surrender to Christ as you pray through them.

This book is intended to build your walk with Jesus Christ. It can be read in one sitting as an immersion experience. It can also be read as a 31-day devotional. I encourage doing both. The experience of a continuous read will take you deep into an encounter with the Christ who calls us to surrender to His strength rather than living by our own. Going on to read it through as a devotional will allow time for processing and prayer in between each chapter. This approach will help you to build new foundations into your life as the Spirit of

God equips you with practical tools to follow Him in the life He has called you to.

If you are a new believer, these devotionals will help you set the tone for your relationship with Him. If you are a seasoned believer, these devotionals will affirm you in a walk of ongoing surrender. If you are coming out of a legalistic or performance-based type of religious experience, these devotionals will help you reframe how you view God, empowering you to walk a journey of freedom rather than one of guilt and failure.

Be blessed as you walk in the grace of Jesus Christ!

Boyd Hopkins

Day 1

The Two Most Important Things

A man came to Jesus and asked:

> *"'Teacher, which is the great commandment in the Law?' And
> He said to him, 'You shall love the Lord your God with all
> your heart, and with all your soul, and with all your mind.'
> This is the great and foremost commandment. The second is
> like it, 'You shall love your neighbor as yourself.' On these two
> commandments depend the whole Law and the Prophets."*
>
> *Matthew 22:36-40*

Jesus teaches that God desires, above all else, to bring about two
things in our lives. First, He desires to restore the relationship
between Himself and us for which we were created. Secondly, He
seeks to restore our ability to have the kind of healthy relationships
with each other that He intended us to have. Every touch of God
in our lives is aimed at drawing us deeper into relationship with
Himself and with each other. God's love for us is His driving motive
and the restoration of these relationships is His goal in everything
He does.

Joe's story

Joe struggled to please God, but the more he worked at it the
less peace he seemed to have. Feeling that he failed more than he
succeeded, with every failure his sense of guilt and shame deepened.
He found himself losing his temper at his wife and children more
and more frequently. As he became increasingly abusive, they began

to pull back from him. Instead of his faith helping him become a better father and husband, the anger he carried over his failed attempts to follow God was making him impossible to live with.

Having come to the point of doubting that he could be used by God at all and fearful that he was losing his faith, Joe sought out a man whom he had heard could really pray. As Joe and Daniel met, Joe poured out his struggle, describing his increasing sense of despair. Daniel listened until Joe was finished. Rather than giving Joe solutions, he simply began to describe God's desire to be in a relationship with Him.

Daniel described a God unlike anything Joe had ever heard of. The God Daniel spoke of was a God of love who desired a relationship rather than demanding perfect performance. His description contrasted sharply with Joe's image of God as a harsh taskmaster who required holy behavior and who threatened punishment when His requirements were not met.

Daniel shared Bible verses that Joe had heard all his life but never in this way. He shared *John 3:16*, emphasizing that God's love for us was the reason that He sent His Son to save us. He spoke of *John 3:17,* where Jesus said that He came to save us rather than to condemn us. He talked about *Romans 5:8* where it says that God loved us so much that He sent Jesus to save us before we could do anything to please Him. He took Joe to *Romans 8:1* and they read together Paul's teaching that, in living a life surrendered to God, we no longer have to live with failure staring us in the face every day.

As Joe listened, something inside him began to soften. The idea that Jesus just wanted a relationship with him touched him deeply and a desire to say "yes" to this God of love began to grow in him. Daniel spoke gently, "You can only give God what you have." With those words, something broke inside Joe. He was ready to say "yes" to Jesus. Convinced that he could do nothing else and finally understanding that in choosing to trust Christ he didn't have to perform anymore, he was ready to let God be God and to just be at His mercy.

Daniel led him in a prayer of surrender. With tears streaming down his face, Joe gave his failure to Jesus along with his sense of guilt and self-hatred. Peace he had never known before engulfed him. So this is what being forgiven was really like!

At the end of the prayer, they sat immersed in the silence. Into that quiet moment, Daniel spoke, "What are you experiencing?" Joe looked at Daniel out of tear-filled eyes, "Peace." Daniel told Joe that the peace he was experiencing was a fruit of the Spirit *(Galatians 5:22-23)*. It was evidence that God had answered his prayer.

Joe went home. Right away, Joe's family began to notice changes in him. As she watched cautiously, his wife was impressed enough that she asked him to begin sharing what he had learned during his time with Daniel. They began reading their Bible together. As they learned to pray and study together, their relationship began to turn around. New intimacy, forgiveness, and trust began to grow in their relationship as they sought God together.

Jesus said that the most important thing to God is that we come to love Him. He went on to say that out of loving God will come a secondary call – the call to love each other. The order of these is important because the ability to do the second is created only as we prioritize the first. When Daniel said to Joe, "You can only give what you have," he spoke of *1 John 4:19* where the Apostle John says, "We love, because He first loved us." Jesus understood this truth himself and spent a lot of His time in prayer with His heavenly Father. The love that the Father poured into Him during those times of prayer He later poured into His disciples, as well as to everyone else around Him.

Jesus is our model. If we are going to have what it takes to be in a loving and intimate relationship with a wife, a husband, children, friends, or co-workers – if we are going to have the ability to love others in the way that God created us to – we need to spend time with the source of that love, just as Jesus did.

Loving God is what we were made for. Loving each other is what happens when we give God His place. These are the two relationships that Jesus spoke of when He said, "This is the first and foremost commandment....and the second is like it..."

Just as Joe's failure to love his wife and children gained momentum as he traded away his time with God for his struggle to try to live by the rules he thought God required, the same happens to us when we make the trade-off that Joe made. Our relationship with God is the source of the love we are lacking. In Joe's case, lack of effort was not the problem. He was trying. He just couldn't do it on his own and the constant failure was making him angry and increasingly hard to live with.

We need that surrendered relationship with God. As we spend time with Him, He pours His love into us. In turn, we are empowered to give His love away to others as we serve them in His name. As others experience His love pouring through us, our relationships become increasingly what they were meant to be. Living God's love can never be about our efforts to perform; it can only be about giving away what He has first given us.

Prayer time: Take a minute to quiet your heart and wait on God. Let your focus turn to Jesus.

Pray: Dear Jesus, You say that You love me above all else. I am ready to receive Your love for me. I give You my attempts to please You. I give You my attempts to fix the broken relationships all around me. I give You all the ways I have failed myself, my friends, and my family. I give You all the ways they have failed me. Forgive me for trying to live my life my way and by my strength. I surrender to Your call. I accept Your love for me and the forgiveness of my sins. I give You the relationships in my life that I have not been able to make work and I ask You to let me simply love these people in whatever way they can accept it from me. I am at Your mercy. Lead me into a deepening relationship of love for You and for others, in Jesus' name. Amen.

Day 2

Living the Life of Surrender

"Now after John had been taken into custody, Jesus came into Galilee, preaching the gospel of God, and saying, 'The time is fulfilled, and the kingdom of God is at hand; repent and believe in the gospel.'"

Mark 1:14-15

At the beginning of Jesus' ministry, He preached His central message, a message that would be transformative to those who heard and acted on it. The message of repentance and belief would bring the lost to know their Savior as well as become the foundation of the new lifestyle He would lead them into. It was a call to say "yes" to God's way rather than to their way. It would empower them to live lives based on faith rather than on performance. Beginning with the first time they chose to say "no" to living in their own strength and "yes" to what Christ offered, they would learn to renounce the temptation to go back to their old ways. Day by day, they would move more deeply into a lifestyle of trusting the Spirit of God to lead them through all of life's situations.

The call to repent and believe has several facets. Repentance means exchanging one way of living for another and has both an element of confession and of renunciation. Desperate to exchange what has been destroying them for what will give them life and having come to realize that they aren't able to make the change happen themselves, repentant people are ready to embrace the One who brings change. The good news is that Jesus has come. The One who will save them is here.

Jesus proclaimed that the time is now. Calling all people to renounce self-dependence in favor of God's mercy, the promise of the Gospel was good news for those in need of it. There was deliverance to be had, both from eternal death and from the curse of having to live life in their own strength. Sin had been conquered. God had come to save His children.

All of us who are drawn to repent are ultimately brought to a moment of confession. Both a turning point and a time of getting real, it's a time when we stop trying to hide who we are and what we have done. It's a time of becoming open with ourselves, with God, and, often, with others. In confessing, we acknowledge what has held us in bondage. We get honest about our sin and take responsibility for it. Only as we take responsibility for our sin do we gain the power to give that sin to The One who can save us from it.

An element of renunciation needs to be tied to our confession if repentance is to be complete. Knowing that true change means abandoning what has bound us, we are drawn to renounce what drew us to our sin in the first place, so that we can move beyond its grip on our lives. We are like someone who has taken a mouthful of something we thought might be tasty only to find out that it was poison. In horror, we come to a realization of what we have done and reject our earlier decision. Spewing the poison from our mouths, we know the cost of not doing so.

The way of repentance applies to sins of addiction, control, self-dependence, and deceit, as well as to a host of other things. It could apply to an abuser and that person's abusive lifestyle. It could apply to a codependent person and that person's lifestyle of enabling others to live in unhealthy ways. Regardless of what the sin is, there is a time of realization and a moment of readiness to change that comes to every repentant person. It makes us ready to embrace the freedom Christ offers.

Having called us to repent, Jesus also calls us to believe. Like repentance, believing has two facets as well. To believe means to understand and trust. In bringing us to the place of understanding, the gospel message turns our focus to the Savior Himself. Having fixed our eyes on the Savior, all that remains is to take the step of trust, just as Peter did when he stepped out of the boat in *Matthew 14*.

> *"Peter said to Him, 'Lord, if it is You, command me to come to You on the water.' And He said, 'Come!' And Peter got out of the boat, and walked on the water and came toward Jesus. But seeing the wind, he became frightened, and beginning to sink, he cried out, 'Lord, save me!' Immediately Jesus stretched out His hand and took hold of him, and said to him, 'You of little faith, why did you doubt?'"*
>
> *Matthew 14:28-31*

The story of Peter stepping out of the boat is a story of repentance and belief. In obedience to the call of Jesus, Peter chose to renounce his own abilities in favor of trusting Jesus. Stepping out and walking on the water, he did what he could not have done by his own ability. Then, distracted by his situation, his faith wavered and he took his eyes off Jesus. Back into his own strength, he began to sink. Rather than allow Peter to drown, Jesus caught him and lifted him up. In doing so, He called Peter's focus away from his situation and back to his Savior.

Jesus taught that there is more to repentance and belief than just a one-time prayer that brings eternal life. Repentance and belief are key elements in an ongoing lifestyle of faith, teaching us to live in surrender to the power of God, situation by situation, throughout our daily lives.

Although the call to repent and believe turns our focus back to Christ, it does more. We are called to something deeper than simply verbalizing the words of a prayer. We are called to action. John the Baptist spoke directly about this to a group of well-known religious people who, having heard him preach, wanted to be baptized:

> *"Therefore bear fruit in keeping with repentance; and do not suppose that you can say to yourselves, 'We have Abraham for our father'..."*
>
> *Matthew 3:8-9*

If our repentance and belief go no deeper than words and

participation in religious rituals, John says that we are hypocrites and the faith we say we have is false. Real change comes as we join actions to our words. Positive confession is not enough. Religious heritage is not enough. The actions that follow repentance demonstrate the reality of the surrender and allow the grace and mercy of God to flow into our lives.

Learning to live a lifestyle of repentance and belief is a journey. Unable to change ourselves, our willingness to let God be the God of our situations allows Him to pour His power into our lives repeatedly, convincing us ever more deeply that He is utterly dependable and that we need fear nothing that the world might bring against us.

Call on Him. As Jesus said, the time is at hand. Be real. Take responsibility and give Him your sins and weakness. Spend time with Him daily, confessing any sins that come up. Actively receive His forgiveness and mercy. Actively reject the accusations of the devil who accuses us always. When we take seriously the call to live the lifestyle of repentance and belief, giving Him regular access to our lives, the experience of God's mercy will become familiar to us.

Prayer time: Take a minute and quiet your heart. Sit silently and turn your focus to Jesus. His Spirit is with you.

Pray: Come, Lord Holy Spirit. Search my heart and show me what I hold to myself that You want me to give to You. Show me where I, like Peter, have taken my eyes off You and need to have my focus brought back. I confess that I have sinned and that I am helpless to change myself in my own strength. Jesus, You are the Son of God. You died to destroy the power of my sins to separate me from the love of God. You rose from the dead in victory over all forms of death and oppression. I say "yes" to You today. I give You my sins and accept Your forgiveness and mercy. You are my God and I worship You. My life is now Yours, Lord. Do with me as You will, in Jesus' name. Amen.

Day 3

No One Can Take Them Away

*"My sheep hear My voice, and I know them, and they follow
Me; and I give eternal life to them, and they will never perish;
and no one will snatch them out of My hand. My Father, who
has given them to Me, is greater than all; and no one is able
to snatch them out of the Father's hand. I and the Father are
one."*

John 10:27-30

Christ is a safe place for everyone who is willing to hear His voice.

At a spiritual retreat, a group of young people opened their day with
a time of quietly waiting on God to speak to them. As the time drew
to a close, they were asked to share what they felt God was saying
to them. One young lady shared a vivid picture of Jesus sitting right
by her side, affirming that He was with her in what she was going
through. A young man across the room heard the words, "Be still and
know that I am God." With a wide smile on her face, another young
woman shared, "I just received assurance that He doesn't condemn
me!" When asked if a sense of condemnation was something she had
been struggling with, she responded, "Very much so."

Those few words from the Spirit of God brought to the group
a sense of belonging, of invitation, and of protection. They had
experienced the presence of Jesus the Good Shepherd. They had
heard His voice. Affirmed in their sense of being loved by Him, when
it came time to respond to His call, they did. Some received a sense

of release from the burden they carried, while others gained the simple encouragement that they were not alone.

Jesus specifically used the image of a shepherd and his sheep to describe Himself and those who belong to the family of God. A shepherd is everything to the sheep, just as Jesus wants to become everything that is good to those of us who follow Him. He leads us. He is with us. We are not alone. No longer like a flock of directionless sheep, we have our shepherd who loves us and guides us. Greater than our circumstances, there is no power that can overcome Him and no threat to us that He cannot, or will not, save us from. The thief may come to steal, but our Savior protects us. The devil may try to attack, but Jesus shields us from his assault. The forces of this world may threaten to overwhelm, but, in the midst of it, He is with us. The Good Shepherd takes care of His own.

Jesus says that the sheep respond readily to the shepherd's voice, and so it is with those who follow Christ. When He speaks, his voice resonates in the hearts of those who belong to Him. Having come to know Him, we also come to rest in the sense that He loves us. We follow Him where He leads us just because He has asked us to. Obedience is not an issue for a sheep that knows he is loved. This sheep simply assumes that the shepherd knows what he is doing and that whatever it is, it is best. He gets up and follows.

There is an attraction to the Good Shepherd, Jesus. There is something that draws His people to want to be in His presence. He comes to lead those who belong to Him. Like lambs, we wander off at times, but Jesus, like the shepherd, comes after us. Often, even before we know we are in trouble, He is already seeking us out. Refusing to give up on us, He calls us and keeps us safe. He doesn't leave us to find our way out of trouble on our own, nor are we left to fix our own mistakes, because that is what the shepherd is for. Under His protection, the lambs know real freedom, a real sense of safety and an absence of fear. They can rest.

Pray: Father, I take my rest this morning in Your hands. I accept Your protection from every power that would come against me this day. I stand under the blood covering of Jesus, my Lord. I listen for the sound of Your voice. I know that today there will be many voices speaking to me and many forces tugging at me. I also know that my challenge will be to rest in You and not try to take on the responsibility of saving myself, and the family I belong to, from an uncertain future. Lord, I believe that You hold the future as You hold me and the family that You have blessed me with. I also know that You can make Your voice heard above the "everything else" that competes for my attention. I know that Your protection will overcome every threat, and I entrust myself, along with all that concerns me, into Your hands for this day. Thank You for the family I belong to. Let Your voice speak into their lives as well, in Jesus' name. Amen.

Day 4

God's Elect

"Peter, an apostle of Jesus Christ, to God's elect, exiles scattered throughout the provinces of Pontus, Galatia, Cappadocia, Asia and Bithynia..."

1 Peter 1:1 (NIV)

Peter wrote to "God's elect." "Elect" means "chosen." He is speaking to those of us who have responded to the Holy Spirit's call to give our lives in service to Christ. It is no accident that we have come to know Him, or that we yearn to know Him more deeply, because He Himself is actively drawing us to Himself.

Jesus said, *"No one can come to Me except that the Father who sent Me draws him..."* or her, as the case may be *(John 6:44)*. Understanding this powerful reality has rattled my world in the past year. I am chosen. I don't have to find out what God wants of me on my own. He will lead me into it and empower me as I follow His calling.

God chooses us and draws us with a purpose. His call first invites us to receive salvation from eternal darkness, but there is more. God is purposeful with regard to my life, and with regard to yours. Desiring so much more than just having us do something for Him, He wants to do something through us. There is a significant difference between the two understandings.

If we live with an emphasis on doing stuff for God, we will fail for two reasons. The first is because our strength, in itself, is inadequate for the task. The second reason is that our understanding, clouded by our limited perspective of what we should do along with our tendency to be self-serving, is likely to be mistaken. But if we live in yieldedness to God, God Himself lives in us, accomplishing His work through us by His strength, and leading us in our understanding of how to live out the purpose He has called us to. Where we may fail, He can never fail, because He is all powerful.

Jesus said to His disciples:

> *"You did not choose me, but I chose you and appointed you that you would go and bear fruit, and that your fruit would remain, so that whatever you ask of the Father in My name He may give to you."*
>
> *John 15:16*

God declares His intent for our lives. As we walk in surrender to His call on our life, God will use us to bear fruit for His kingdom. He will teach us how to pray and then give us what we ask, so that we can be effective in serving Him. The impact we will have, the legacy we will leave, will be an eternal one.

In Galatians, the Apostle Paul said that good fruit comes through the Spirit who works and lives in us *(Galatians 5:22-23)*. He speaks of the fruit that comes as we live by the Spirit and abandon living by the strength of our flesh.

Jesus' last word to His disciples before he was taken up into heaven, in Luke 24:49, was to wait! Waiting for the promise of God's Spirit, they would be clothed with the power of the Holy Spirit. Only then could they venture forth to serve Him.

Jesus' disciples obeyed and waited. When the Spirit came upon them, God's power began to pour through them. They became agents of God's change in the society around them. Leading them out into the world in the power of the Spirit, God, in His love for the lost, began to call many more to eternal life through them. We, who follow Christ today, are some of the fruit that Jesus promised them they would bear. There is more fruit to come. Some of it will come through you and through me.

Pray: Heavenly Lord, I acknowledge today that I am one of Your chosen ones. You have called me and drawn me to Yourself with a purpose. You know what You want to do with me. I accept that, like Your first disciples, I have been given an anointing to serve You simply because You have chosen me, called me, and poured Your Spirit out on my life. I trust that You will empower me for that service. By Your grace, I will bear good fruit and fruit that will last. Father, I ask and receive Your forgiveness for the times when I have attempted to serve You in my own strength and failed. I receive Your forgiveness for trying to live for You out of my own strength and for allowing my failures to cause me to lose faith in Your desire to use me. I accept that You cannot fail me and I surrender my life into Your loving hands. I wait on You today. Clothe me with Your power. Take my life and use me for Your purpose. Bear the fruit of the kingdom in me. I am in Your hands in, in Jesus' name. Amen.

Day 5

Scattered Strangers

"To the strangers scattered throughout Pontus, Galatia, Cappadocia, Asia, and Bithynia..."

1 Peter 1:1 (KJV)

Scattered strangers no longer fit this life in the way they once did.

A friend in the business community surrendered his life to Christ some time ago. Giving his life to Christ did more than give him hope for eternity, it caused significant changes in the way he lived and did business. As we talked about it one day, he shared, "I don't know how I am going to be able to continue to work in this industry. I used to do and say what I had to in order to get the business, but I don't think I can work that way anymore. I'm not sure how I am going to adapt being a Christian to that kind of environment."

As a brand-new believer, my friend was already beginning to experience that surrender to Christ brings more than eternal life. It also brings a calling to carry the message of Christ into the world we live in. God doesn't wait for us to change on our own. He implants in us new values and priorities by the power of the Holy Spirit. Motivated and empowered by the Spirit of Jesus Christ who now lives in us and who yearns to express Himself through us, old ethics are replaced by the ethics of Jesus. Old, dishonest, and manipulative ways have to give way to a lifestyle based on a new integrity. With the motives that once directed the way we lived beginning to change and demanding that we make changes in the way we interact with our world, the old ways no longer work for us.

This is the way it was with my friend. The old, sinful ways of doing business that had once been second nature to my friend were no longer natural for him, because Christ had changed him. He was now different. He no longer fit the lifestyle and business world that he was used to. Anyone who says "yes" to the call of Christ, and surrenders their life to Him, will experience the same. We no longer fit the old way of living. In Romans 6, Paul asks a question:

> *"We are those who have died to sin; how can we live in it any longer?"*
>
> *Romans 6:2 (NIV)*

The straightforward response to Paul's question is that we can't. Yet often we forget this, spending our time and energy as we try to shoehorn ourselves into a lifestyle that no longer works for us.

God brings change to us by the power of Christ's Spirit. As His Spirit collides with our old lifestyle, He begins to uproot our old values along with the self-centered motives that used to drive us. The longer we follow Him, the more we begin to sense that life is no longer all about us, nor is it even about the few years we have here on this earth. We find a new perspective - an eternal perspective - changing the way that we look at the people we work and play with. Do they know that life is about more than clothes and cars and getting the next business deal done? Do they know that they have eternal worth and that God is calling them? Are they aware of the importance of being "in Christ" when they cross the threshold of death and enter eternity?

God very purposefully embeds His message of good news within those of us who serve Him. One of the last things He said to His disciples was that they were to go into all the world and to carry His message with them as they went *(Matthew 28:19-20)*. Then He scattered them across the then-known world over a period of time known as The Great Dispersion.

Just as God sent out the first disciples, God continues to send out those who say "yes" to His calling. God knows how He wants to use us and that we cannot be effective for Him as long as we try to fit in with the way the world works. To that end, He empowers us to proclaim the message of Christ by filling us with the power of the Holy Spirit *(Acts 1:8),* and He scatters us, placing us where we can bring His message to those in need of it. Due to the way He has changed us, we are definitely a strange people. No longer able to endorse the values and practices of our world context, and contrasting with the society around us, we stand out like a light in a dark place. Those who are hungry for the light we carry will be drawn to us, seeking the message we bring through our words and by our lifestyle.

In choosing to actively let go of who we were, and in embracing who we have become in Christ, we acknowledge that we don't belong here anymore, even though we still live and work here. We are strangers who have been scattered according to the Father's will. We are where He has placed us. We have a calling. We have a message!

Pray: Dear Lord, I acknowledge that I do not fit this world. Forgive me for the times when I have tried to fit in and have tried to use the world's ways. I give You my dissatisfaction with the values that this world promotes. I accept Your calling to be a "scattered stranger." Take me where You will. Use me as You want. Fill my heart with Your perspective. I want to see the world, and others, the way You do. I want to make an impact in the place You have me right now. Use me there by the power of Your Spirit, in Jesus' name. Amen!

Day 6

This Is My Prayer

"And this I pray, that your love may abound still more and more in real knowledge and all discernment, so that you may approve the things that are excellent, in order to be sincere and blameless until the day of Christ; having been filled with the fruit of righteousness, which comes through Jesus Christ, to the glory and praise of God."

Philippians 1:9-11

According to Jesus, two commands sum up Christ-like living. We are called to love God and to love each other as we love ourselves *(Matthew 22:37-40).*

Paul prays for us to receive a love like Christ, deeper than what we are used to, abounding in knowledge and discernment. Abound means "to increase," "to overflow," and "to have more than you need." Discernment means "depth of insight." Having this kind of love allows us to understand why people do some of the difficult things that they do and to love them anyway. This includes learning to love ourselves as well, regardless of our failings.

It is tough to love others unless we love ourselves. How can we give away something that we don't have and, if we are lacking it, how do we get it in the first place? In *1 John 4:19,* it says, "We love, because He has first loved us." We first need to be exposed to God's unconditional love for us, because we get our ability to love directly from God Himself.

There is something life changing about unconditional love. When we are loved without condition, our failures and the things we hate about ourselves get washed away in our amazement at how we are valued by the one who loves us. To someone at least, we are worth everything. When we are in their presence, we have a sense that our value is unquestionable and that to them we are a pleasure to be with. Happy to be with us, they change our lives with their love.

Exposure to love like this is transforming. In experiencing God's love for us, we become aware that we bring joy to the heart of God, not because of what we do, but because of who we are. In being exposed to the heart of God and experiencing His love for us, we are set free from the fear of making mistakes, because we know He will love us regardless of how we stumble. The overflow of that freedom manifests itself in our lives as we become able to love others out of what we have received from God Himself.

Paul prayed that this love we have received from God would abound in knowledge and depth of insight, so that we could know what is excellent and that our love could be pure and unselfish. We don't have to be fake or put on masks in order to be loved by God. His love calls us to be honest and real about who we are. Growing in the love of God, we come to know ourselves, our needs, our tendencies, and the inner motives that affect the way we relate to God and to one another. Knowing that we have the freedom to be who we are in the presence of God sets the stage for how Paul prays that we will come to love each other.

Paul knew that we would need to love others with our eyes open if we are to truly love as Jesus did.

In other words, our love is not blind.

Healthy and godly love is not stupid. It does not demand that we wear masks, pretending to be someone we are not. It does not equate the sinner with his sin, overlooking destructive behavior because of a co-dependent need to affirm each other or a fear of what being honest will do to the relationship. It does not manipulate, demanding we prove our love by doing whatever is asked of us regardless of the consequence to those around us. Christ-like love allows us to stand firm in what we have come to know as the truth.

Understanding that healthy relationships thrive on truth allows us to be real with each other and with God. Hearts connect intimately in relationships where it is okay to be who we are with each other.

Jesus loved, but He never facilitated evil behavior. He was never manipulated, although many people tried to do so. Always offering forgiveness, He also confronted unhealthy behavior in those to whom He ministered. As our love deepens in knowledge, we come to understand that many people live with brokenness and that people who are broken tend to live out of their brokenness. In being called to develop the ability to know the difference between healthy behavior and unhealthy behavior, God allows us to grow in our ability to love without validating actions that are destructive to the relationship.

As our love deepens in discernment and insight, we develop in our ability to recognize healthy and unhealthy behavior. As we become increasingly aware of the selfish motives in ourselves and in those we love, it becomes easier for us to recognize attempts to manipulate and to abuse. In developing the ability to recognize actions that stem from brokenness, we are less prone to respond reactively and more able to be proactive. In giving us insight, the Holy Spirit leads us to take action. The leading He gives will always be in the best interests of the relationship.

As we grow in His ways, God leads us in loving unconditionally and in loving wisely, just as Jesus did. This "wise" love results in peace for those who practice it *(Galatians 5:22)*. As we learn to make allowances for others' failures, we also learn to make allowances for our own failures as well. As we grow in our ability to set boundaries on unhealthy relationships, we learn to say "no" to those who act in unhealthy ways, without taking our love back. Like Jesus, we learn to allow people to live their own lives and make their own choices without having to control them. We can love even as we take our stand for what is good and healthy.

Pray: Dear Jesus, show me Your heart and transform me. Today I accept Your love for me. I accept that I am deeply valuable to You. Forgive me for the times I have hated myself, because I know that such self-hatred has prevented me from receiving Your love and

from loving myself and others. Teach me the depth and insight of
Your love. Help me to love unconditionally and yet wisely. Lord,
I need Your wisdom, so that I can set healthy boundaries in my
relationships. Let me know what is best, so that I can make the
healthy choices that I need to make. I love You, Lord, in Jesus' name.
Amen.

Day 7

I Know That This will Turn Out Well

"...for I know that this will turn out for my deliverance through your prayers and the provision of the Spirit of Jesus Christ, according to my earnest expectation and hope, that I will not be put to shame in anything, but that with all boldness, Christ will even now, as always, be exalted in my body, whether by life or by death."

Philippians 1:19-20

Paul was in trouble. He had been arrested and was in prison under threat of death. For most of us, this would be a good time to panic, but not Paul. He had confidence in the midst of a bad situation. How did he get such confidence? I need some of that!

People with confidence naturally express the hope they have. With a sense that beyond their circumstances something bigger is coming, they may not know exactly what will happen, but they know that God has everything in hand regardless. Anticipating something good to come, they are on the watch for that good thing, whatever it is. They know they will recognize it when they see it and they are prepared to receive what God brings. This confident expectancy is what *Hebrews 11:1 (KJV)* calls "the substance of things hoped for." It is faith! The writer of Hebrews 11:6 goes on to say that faith (confidence in God's provision) pleases God, because this "confidence" enables us to receive what He wants to give us.

God loves it when His children receive what He offers them!

It is different with people who live without confidence.

People who live without confidence live without joy. With no sense of hope for the future, they live steeped in a potent mix of fear and despair as they dread what lies ahead. Fear and despair, if left long enough, open the way for anger to rule their lives. Anxiety gradually takes over as situations, coupled with their sense of helplessness, spiral beyond their control. They may "turtle up," going into survival mode, or they may live with a hatred of the past, because, in their minds, what happened "back then" has brought them to where they are now – living without hope.

People without hope may yearn for the past, feeling that, if they only had another chance, they wouldn't make the same mistakes again and all would be well. They may obsess over the "if only." "If only I had done something different," or "If only God had done something different," or "If only my life hadn't gone in the direction it has taken."

People without hope live with anger, because their expectations of life and relationships have failed. Chronic disappointment makes for miserable, angry people. Invariably, to people who live without hope, their situation is all that they can see. Unable to see beyond their situation to God, who has the power to bring something good out of it, neither can they receive the peace that He offers to those who trust Him.

Paul saw beyond his situation. Having deeply experienced the grace of God, his faith had grown into a confidence that God was in control regardless of how the situation looked. It didn't matter to him that things were tough in the moment, because he knew that God was absolutely faithful and would only take him into hard places in order to do something good.

God had a call on Paul's life and Paul said "yes" to that calling. Having gained his confidence by the simple and yet radical expedient of putting his daily living into the hands of God's Holy Spirit, Paul told God, "My life is Yours to do with as You will." Taking Paul at his word, God began to use him to spread the message of hope that we know as the good news of Christ. Paul's job in the situation was simply to trust God. Ours is the same.

The world is often hostile to the message of Christ and that hostility can mean consequences for the one who brings the message. Over and over, God took Paul into places and situations where only the Holy Spirit could save him. In those places, people saw the power of God demonstrated and the Gospel advanced. Helpless, according to worldly standards, Paul was always at someone's mercy and in way over his head. Yet, because Paul was willing to go to those places with God, he experienced the trustworthiness and the faithfulness of God as God demonstrated His power in Paul's predicament. Out of that wealth of experience Paul writes, "I have confidence – confidence in my God who has never let me down; confidence in my God who has carried me through every circumstance that has been too big for me."

Paul had learned, as had John, to look beyond the situation to the Savior, and to say, *"Come, Lord Jesus!" (Revelation 22:20).*

What if you find yourself in a hopeless situation, or living with an accumulation of hopeless situations? How do you get this confidence that Paul had? I would like to say that you just need to read your Bible, absorb the principles, and apply them. The reality, however, is much more intense.

It is a difficult truth that those of us who follow Christ only gain this kind of faith by allowing God to take us into the places where we are not in control. There we gain the experience of God's faithfulness. There we experience our helplessness as God prepares us to trust Him, having left us nowhere else to turn but to Him. There we gain the ability to say "Amen!" to God's saving power. It's not an easy process. In fact, Jesus likens it to dying – dying to ourselves in order that we may live in Christ *(Mark 8:35).*

Are you ready?

Pray: *Dear Father in Heaven. Hallowed be Your name.* I worship You. Your kingdom come. I say "yes" to Your power and renounce living by my own strength. Your will be done. I give myself to Your purposes and renounce my own demands and plans for my life and situation.

Give me today my daily provision. Lord, I trust You for all I need. You are my provider and I acknowledge that I cannot gain my own provision aside from You.

Forgive me as I forgive others who have hurt me. I give You my anger over all of the betrayal and failed expectations in my life and relationships. Lord, I receive Your forgiveness for being so self-absorbed.

Lead me not into temptation and deliver me from the evil one. Lord, I know that nothing evil comes from You. Forgive me for the times I have blamed You for my situations. I know that the evil one, Satan, would seek to bind me in despair. Forgive me for the times I have believed his lies rather than Your Word. Heavenly Lord, You are my deliverer and I receive my freedom from Your hand.

The kingdom, the power, and the glory are Yours, now and forever! Keep this always before me in every situation. You are greater than anything I can encounter or anything that might threaten to overwhelm me. I accept a new confidence in You and I look forward to what You will bring. In Jesus' name, I pray. Amen.

Day 8

And I Will Continue to Rejoice

"Yes, and I will continue to rejoice, for I know that through your prayers and God's provision of the Spirit of Jesus Christ, what has happened to me will turn out for my deliverance. I eagerly expect and hope that I will in no way be ashamed, but will have sufficient courage so that now as always Christ will be exalted in my body, whether by life or by death."

Philippians 1:18-20 (NIV)

Paul's rejoicing reflected a lifestyle choice he had made in response to God's call on his life. It came from a determination to keep on rejoicing regardless of what happened. It was a Spirit-empowered decision to keep his hope in Christ rather than being distracted by the evident hopelessness of the situation he was in – a situation that was greater than he could deal with by his own gifts and strength.

This is what *Hebrews 13:15* called a "sacrifice of praise to God...the fruit of lips that give thanks to His name!"

True rejoicing is a kind of waiting on God and is often a choice we make rather than a feeling we follow. As we grow deeper in our walk with Christ, we learn to make the choice to rejoice that Paul made. Rejoicing not just because we have seen God work, we rejoice because we know that He will work. Even when we do not understand what He is doing, we trust that whatever He chooses will be the best both for us and for those He is using us to reach.

Paul anticipated the godly outcome of his situation and acted on that anticipation by rejoicing as an act of faith. Praising God for what he did not yet see, he had an unshakeable conviction that God would work for his deliverance, knowing that God glorifies Himself by pouring Himself into this world through the prayers of His people.

Paul describes a "Holy Partnership" with God. Paul saw this partnership, comprising the prayers of the believers and the help of the Spirit, as being crucial for his deliverance. Knowing that we, too, are called to this partnership is necessary if we are to deliberately walk in step with the leading of the Spirit. Recognizing prayer as a part of our partnership with God readies us to receive His grace. More than a symbolic act that we do because God likes to watch us do it, our prayers are effective because they turn us toward God in faith. Enabling us to exert the authority of Christ on this earth, prayer is part of our service to God.

Thank God that living for Him is not something left up to us alone. Partnered with God, I will rejoice!

Pray: Dear Lord, I rejoice in the place of life where You have me. I know that You will empower me to keep my focus on You and to glorify Your name. I know that You do not leave me in the hands of the enemy. Lord, I trust You as my protector. You are my deliverer, so I give myself to You and expect Your mercy and provision. Lord, I know people who are struggling and who are in danger of feeling overwhelmed. I name them before You now: _______________________________. Call me to regular prayer for them, so that they can experience Your mercy and deliverance as well. Bring us together some day to share the stories of Your deliverance and to rejoice in You. In Jesus' name, I pray. Amen.

Day 9

I Am Torn

*"I eagerly expect and hope that I will in no way be ashamed,
but will have sufficient courage so that now as always Christ
will be exalted in my body, whether by life or by death. For to
me, to live is Christ and to die is gain. If I am to go on living in
the body, this will mean fruitful labor for me. Yet what shall I
choose? I do not know! I am torn between the two: I desire to
depart and be with Christ, which is better by far; but it is more
necessary for you that I remain in the body. Convinced of this,
I know that I will remain, and I will continue with all of you
for your progress and joy in the faith, so that through my being
with you again your boasting in Christ Jesus will overflow on
account of me."*

Philippians 1:20-26 (NIV)

Our family had all known my grandmother as a quiet and gentle
woman. Whenever she came to visit, she darned every sock in the
house that she could find with a hole in it - this in a day and age of six
pairs for $6.99. I haven't had a sock darned since.

Grandma was wonderful. She caught us boys more than once in our
shenanigans but we never got a condemning word from her. She
always had a smile, an open door, and a little something for us to
eat. By her actions, I would have said she was Christ-like, definitely a
Christian, if a Christian can be known by his or her lifestyle. Never
aggressive about her faith, nor overly vocal, we knew her relationship
with God was there, quiet and constant.

Until the weeks before her death.

Something happened to Grandma once she got to the hospital. Knowing that her time had come, she was ready for it. In fact, she was more than ready. She yearned for heaven. Like Paul, she had a deep desire to depart and be with Christ her Savior. She was tired of here and wanted to be there where *"He will wipe every tear from their eyes. There will be no more death or mourning or crying or pain, for the old order of things has passed away"* (Revelation 21:4 NIV).

But she was torn. She had a sense that she was not finished here – yet.

Unable to be with Grandma in those final weeks, family members shared with me the story of her last days. She made it clear that she knew some of her grandchildren had little in the way of a faith in God. To many of us, Jesus was a Sunday school story and not much else. As the time of her departure from this earth came near, Grandma gained a deep sense of calling. She felt God telling her that she couldn't go home until she had prayed for every one of her grandchildren in person – grandchildren whom she felt needed to know more of God's love for them. Torn between her yearning to go and be with God and her deep sense of the need to pray with each grandchild, she sent the word out through the family, along with a list of names. "Bring them to me!" One by one, they were brought and, as they came, she prayed for them.

I don't just mean that she mumbled over them in the name of Jesus either. She prayed both out loud and with volume. With the courage of Christ flowing through her body, soul, and spirit, there was no fear or shyness. She demanded to see each grandchild from the list she had given. As they were brought to her, she took hold of them and prayed for their salvation. She cried out to God on their behalf while they stood stunned and awestruck in the presence of this little old woman of humility, who had suddenly been transformed into a mighty woman of God, filled with faith and power.

Like Paul, Grandma was torn. Her time on earth was finished. With heaven so close and this life no longer worth trying to hold onto, she had something that few people gain – a healthy hunger for eternity that consumed all else to the point that all worldly fears were wiped out. With nothing to lose and everything to gain, she could sense the nearness of God and she wanted to go to Him.

After the funeral, I found a group of my cousins gathered together and talking in subdued tones. We spoke of never having seen anything like it. She had assaulted heaven on our behalf. She had cried out to God for our salvation. She had exhorted us to believe and, when the last one had come to see her, she turned her eyes to heaven, reaching up with frail, shaking arms and started to shout, "Come get me!" She went to be with Jesus shortly thereafter.

People confront death differently. When there is no sense of an imminent death, few actually treat life here as though it were a springboard to eternity.

But it is.

Paul knew that. My Grandma knew it, too, in the last days of her life. That knowledge was so powerful to her that caution and propriety were thrown to the wind in her urgency to pass on her faith in Jesus before she went to be with Him.

Not everyone reacts like Grandma did to the knowledge that they are dying. People react in a variety of ways when they know that the time of their death has come upon them.

Some react in terror. Not knowing what lies ahead, they fear what is unknown to them. Death is to be ignored and avoided at all cost, because to face it means having to face the fear of what awaits beyond the grave, and they know that they are not ready to do that.

Some react by struggling to live. Knowing that heaven awaits but, having spent so little time with the Lord and so much time in the world, they struggle and strive to hang onto this life for as long as possible. In a fight to the last, they battle death as though it is their enemy. Though they may not believe that death is the end, they certainly have no yearning for it as Grandma and Paul did.

Others embrace death as an escape. Their focus consumed with escaping a world that has overcome them, there is no thought of eternity, only of finding a way out of the pain of living. Families of these people often find themselves shocked and grief stricken over a call describing the abrupt suicide of their loved one.

Some, filled with anticipation, react as Grandma and Paul did. Through eyes of faith, they view death not as something to be avoided but as a gateway to heaven - the fulfillment of a life lived for Christ. In the moment of knowing that their time has come, they see all that is yet to be done and are drawn to abandon the fight for self and to live for Christ through their last moments of life. Caution thrown aside, and with no care for appearances, only Jesus matters now - Jesus and those with whom the message of salvation and hope still needs to be shared.

Paul was convinced that God would keep him on earth because there was more that he had to do for the kingdom. God was not done with him. Grandma, too, sensed a call to remain awhile. Knowing what she had to do, she did it. Having fulfilled her purpose, she went to be with Jesus.

What about us? Each of us will face death. Understanding that for those who have said "yes" to Jesus, God has our eternal future in His hands, there is more to do. Together, and by His Spirit's empowering presence, we are called to live as though we will never die and, at the same time, to share our faith in Christ as though it is our last day of life on this earth.

Pray: Show me, Lord! Show me the perspective on my life that You showed to Paul and Grandma. Open my eyes. Let me live this life as though it were a springboard for the next. I renounce yearning for death as an escape from this life. I renounce getting so caught up in this life that I have forgotten what my eternal calling is. I let go of life as I have come to expect and desire it. I give the life I have to You. I am convinced that You want to use me and so I say "yes" to You. I renounce the lies and distractions of the world, the flesh, and the devil, and I accept the high calling of God. Fill me with Your Spirit. Open my eyes to follow You. In Jesus' mighty name, I pray. Amen.

Day 10

Make My Joy Complete

"If you have any encouragement from being united with Christ, if any comfort from his love, if any common sharing in the Spirit, if any tenderness and compassion, then make my joy complete by being like-minded, having the same love, being one in spirit and of one mind. Do nothing out of selfish ambition or vain conceit. Rather, in humility value others above yourselves, not looking to your own interests, but each of you to the interests of the others."

Philippians 2:1-4 (NIV)

A paraphrase of the above verses might go something like this, "If you are really the family of God, make my joy complete by living your love for one another as Christ lived His love for you."

For those who have said "yes" to Jesus, the scriptures teach us that we are family. Like many families, often what others see in public is not the same as what goes on in private. We often treat each other with less civility than we treat visitors. When our family was young, I remember many of our babysitters saying how wonderful and perfect our children were. Looking at each other, my wife and I would graciously receive the compliments. Afterwards we'd laugh, asking each other, "Are these the same children we know?" Obviously what the children had shown the babysitters was not the same kind of interaction they normally showed each other when we were alone together at home.

Young parents soon come to realize that no amount of logic can make family members behave civilly toward each other all the time. Logic often gets lost as interests collide and siblings tussle to get their way. It is like giving gifts to my children. No kind of strategic purchasing can make everyone satisfied with the toys they get. Nor does it prevent competition as one child, instead of saying "thank you" for what was just given to her, voices dissatisfaction with what she received and tries to lay claim to a sibling's gift.

Growth without conflict. In our family, we have come to believe that it can't be done. That said, there are certain things that I would say we are all united on. Family pizza night is one, and time together after school is another. Hangout time is a priority regardless of the activity we engage in.

My wife and I have discovered that our children actually do love each other, even though their treatment of one another has sometimes made us wonder. When they play together, they often play actively and well. When they disagree, they are always very open about their feelings and thoughts, to the point that they are sometimes a little too free in accusing each other of wrongdoing.

Our children don't cover much up, but we have found that, if one of them truly is hurting, they all hurt to some degree. If one loses something and is heartbroken over the loss, they will gather around in order to comfort the one struggling with the loss, as well as to figure out a way to replace whatever it was. Though often lacking in maturity, they do love each other and have a common sense of identity as brothers and sisters. Learning to express that unity in a way that is uplifting to the family is the growth curve that we are on together.

Generic children? I think not! On the contrary, they are each quite unique. One in family and one in love for each other? Yes! Mature? Not at all! On the journey of growth and maturity? Yes, again! Needing some coaching in that journey of growth? Absolutely!

Parents take joy in seeing their children learning to be loving and real with each other. While that journey of growth includes moments of self-centeredness, it also includes times when we have the privilege of seeing them lay self-interests aside in order to grow together in resolving issues and in learning to deal with offences and hurts. Growth means more than just adding people to the family. It means deepening relationships. Like any healthy parent, God takes joy in seeing us grow in relationship with each other.

Refusing to make appearances the priority among His children, God's top priority for his family is growth. Sweeping aside the plastic veneer of having it all together when, in reality, there are struggles among us, God calls us to be real with him and with each other. Teaching us to take the risks of being honest and transparent with each other, He gives us a sense of belonging to one another that is greater than our differences. When new additions to the family are made (as happens when someone comes to know Christ), He teaches us how to have patience with those who are immature while at the same time helping them to grow in their new faith.

In a growing family, there is no demand for perfection, because everyone knows that none of us is capable of it.

For those who are a part of the family of God, our common identity is based on our relationship with Jesus. Called to unity in Spirit, Paul leaves no doubt as to the identity of the unifying Spirit. Much more than a simple attitude, or "spirit," He is the Holy Spirit, the Spirit of Jesus the Risen Christ. Encouraging us as a body of believers to take our shared identity seriously, Paul calls us to become active in our relationship with one another. Just as children learn a sense of community in a family context, we learn to be followers of Christ in the family-of-God context. As we serve alongside others in our shared relationship with Christ, and in the Spirit who expresses Himself among us, we grow in relationship as the family of God. Not made to walk this walk alone, we need each other.

The needs among us quickly become obvious, as does our calling to serve one another. Learning to put our own needs last as Jesus did, we give of ourselves in order to bring encouragement to each other. In choosing to get real and in taking the risks that getting real entails, we renounce selfishness and conceit. In looking out for the other person's needs rather than just our own, we come to experience that our health and joy are tied to the health and joy of the rest of our faith family, and we come to love one another as Christ has loved us

(Ephesians 5:2).

That kind of family living gives a parent joy. It gave Paul joy. It gives God joy.

Pray: Dear Jesus, open my eyes to the needs around me in the family of God. I ask You to help me grow and to lead me in laying down my own selfish interests, situation by situation, as I learn to serve my brothers and sisters in Christ. I ask for Your awareness, so that I can see when and where I may be of service. I want to participate in the unity of the Spirit with other believers. I want to know that I belong and I want to help others know that they belong and are cared for. Lord, I want to give You joy, in Jesus' name. Amen.

Day 11

Have This Attitude

"Have the same mindset as Christ Jesus: Who, being in very nature God, did not consider equality with God something to be used for his own advantage; rather, he made himself nothing, taking the very nature of a servant, being made in human likeness. And being found in appearance as a man, he humbled himself by becoming obedient to death – even death on a cross!"

Philippians 2:5-8 (NIV)

Jesus was determined not to claim His rights, choosing instead to live and die selflessly. An enigma to many who met Him, they could not understand why He would do what He was doing. In *John 19:9-11 (NIV)*, Pontius Pilate bluntly asked Him to defend His rights. *"Where do you come from?" he asked Jesus. Jesus gave him no answer. "Do you refuse to speak to me?" Pilate said. "Don't you realize I have power either to free you or to crucify you"? Jesus' response was short, "You would have no power over me if it were not given to you from above."* Having said that much, Jesus would say no more. Keeping His mouth shut and refusing to defend Himself against the accusations that the Pharisees and Sadducees brought against Him, He sealed his fate. His silence would take Him to the cross of Calvary.

In praying about this passage one day, it struck me that there would have been enormous consequences for all of us had Jesus chosen His own rights over doing what His Heavenly Father asked Him to do. Had He simply told Pilate the truth - that the charges against Him were false - He would have been freed. Had He been freed, the cross and the resurrection would not have taken place, payment for the sins of the world would not have been made, and all humanity would have been doomed to an eternity apart from God.

For this reason, Jesus kept His mouth shut. Refusing to claim His rights and driven by His love for both His Father and for us, He laid down all of His privileges as the Son of God in order to accomplish something greater – the salvation of humanity.

I have learned this about the walk with Jesus: "God is not about fair. God is about mercy."

If God was about "fair," I'd get what I deserve and would be going to Hell right now.

This realization drew me to the question of my own rights. I do have rights and so have we all. Can we demand them? Yes. Are we equal in value to others? Absolutely. Yet the Bible teaches us that there is something greater to give ourselves to than a lifestyle of grasping for those rights and proving our equality. In being called to imitate Jesus, we are called to lay down our rights. The Holy Spirit leads us into a lifestyle of refusing to demand our equality in order that the love of Christ may be poured into someone else's life through our Christ-like self-sacrifice. Jesus is our model. Equal to God the Father and with all the rights that heaven could offer, He laid them aside, so that He could make mercy His central focus.

Jesus was equal to the Heavenly Father. Paul says so. He refused to demand His divine privileges and the rights that came with that equality. Paul says that, too. Jesus was unselfish. He loved His Heavenly Father more than He loved His sense of equality and that love drove Him to act without a demand for "rights" as His guiding motivation. This is so different from the way our society trains us. For us, often, everything is about fair treatment and, until we get it, we just cannot move forward.

Jesus was different. When the Father called, He said "yes" and He went. He did not ask questions. He just did what needed to be done. He trusted the Father. He saw our need. He laid His rights down and obeyed. John 3:16 says that all of this was done for the sake of God's love for us.

When the Father asked Jesus to let go of heaven and come to earth as a helpless human, He said "yes." When the Father asked Him to lay down all of His power and become totally dependent on the Holy Spirit for everything He needed, just like we must do, again He said "yes." When the Father told Him that it was necessary to commit Himself to an earthly journey that would bring Him unjust accusation, rejection, betrayal, and a horrible death, all to pay for the consequences of someone else's sin, Jesus said "yes" to this as well.

This is important to understand for those of us who have said "yes" to Christ. The life we live on this earth will not suddenly become a time of smooth and easy sailing just because we have accepted Jesus. In fact, it will become impossible to live this life successfully out of our own strength and ability. That said, in saying "yes" to Jesus, and in laying down our rights in order to serve Him, He promises to pour His kingdom through us into this world *(Acts 1:8)*.

In saying "yes" to Jesus, we say "yes" to a lifestyle like His. In receiving His calling to give up selfishness for selflessness, we have our eyes increasingly opened, by the compassion of His Spirit, to the self-sacrificing ministry He has for us. Our new lifestyle will cost us something, just as it did Jesus. It will cost us our right to have life as we want it.

For those of us who have said "yes" to Christ, the Father's calling rings through the life, death, and resurrection of Jesus, touching us by the power of the Holy Spirit. With the Spirit leading us to acts of selflessness as He did with Jesus, the Spirit will draw us to yield our hearts to the point where we receive not just His life but His attitude as well. Speaking to us from *1 Corinthians 2:16*, Paul says that we will gain *"the mind of Christ."*

Willingness to exchange our perspective on life for His is essential if we are to embrace a life of surrender to the Spirit of Jesus. As our surrender to Him increasingly pervades our living, we begin to see others around us, along with the situations we find ourselves in, from Jesus' perspective. With Jesus as my master, my life is no longer about me getting my rights. In coming to understand who I have become in Christ, I have come to realize that in my walk with Him there will come situations that require me to surrender my rights if I am going to be used by Him. It changes everything.

Jesus is our model. He laid down His rights at the cross. As His followers, we will be called to the same kind of surrender. In refusing to demand what He could have demanded, He turned His focus to the higher purpose to which He had given Himself. Like Jesus was, we too will be called to give up our demands on life in order that we might participate in something more important.

Jesus humbled Himself. Renouncing His own strength, He regularly cast Himself on the power and mercy of His Father. Humbling ourselves, in the way that Jesus did, means choosing a radical lifestyle that demonstrates trust in God above all else.

How do we live like Jesus did? In accepting the call to humility, we put our trust in a strength that is not our own. True humility has nothing to do with degrading our worth. Truly humble people are not known by how they speak negatively about themselves, but by their trust in God. Speaking poorly of yourself means degrading the person God made you to be and devaluing someone whom Jesus died for. Doing so is sin. A truly humble person learns to simply renounce his or her own personal power and to cast him/herself on the mercy of God, situation by situation. The Spirit of God becomes strength to such a person.

Humility opens the way to a life of faith. Living in humility through trust in God, the Holy Spirit pours God's power through us, equipping us for acts of service and love that both glorify Him and minister His mercy to others.

Prayer time: Take about 60 seconds and relax. Close your eyes and rest in the presence of God.

Pray: Come, Holy Spirit. Dear Jesus, only You fully know the attitudes of my heart that motivate what I do and think. Send Your Spirit upon me. "Search me, O God, and know my heart; try me and know my anxious thoughts; and see if there be any hurtful way in me, and lead me in the everlasting way" *(Psalm 139:23-24)*. I give You __________ (list what God brings to mind). Lord, I surrender to Your Spirit. I give You my attitudes and receive Yours.

Heavenly Lord, I renounce the temptations that the devil would bring to me to be selfish in seeking my own fulfillment in life and I receive the call to serve in Your name. I accept Your blood as my covering and hide myself in You. I love You, in Jesus' name. Amen.

Day 12

He Took the Initiative

"Have the same mindset as Christ Jesus: Who, being in very nature God, did not consider equality with God something to be used for his own advantage; rather, he made himself nothing, taking the very nature of a servant, being made in human likeness. And being found in appearance as a man, he humbled himself by becoming obedient to death – even death on a cross!"

Philippians 2:5-8 (NIV)

Graduating from seminary as a young pastor, I set out to build my ministry. The operative word was "my." Certainly I loved God and wanted to do great things for Him, but, as of yet, I didn't have the attitudes of Jesus as my core motivation for doing what I was called to do. I read many books as I learned how to gather the "cream" of the people around me to help me build "my" ministry. At leadership seminars, we discussed how to come up with vision and mission statements that would enshrine how "we" would do "our" ministries and what "we" wanted to accomplish for the kingdom.

It didn't work out.

Eight years into "my" ministry, I was flat on my back, unemployed, and suffering burnout.

As I took time off to recover, I wondered what had gone wrong. Searching my Bible, I began to see differences between how Jesus led his followers and the leadership flavor of my own training. In

studying Jesus' approach to Christian leadership, I began to learn
about what makes leadership godly as opposed to simply successful.
In getting honest with myself, I had to admit that I had probably
listened to all of this before, but my selfish motives and my desire to
succeed had prevented me from really hearing it.

In reading about how Jesus led, I rediscovered that godly leadership is
not "self" oriented. Rather than looking at people from a "what can
you do for me?" perspective, godly leadership is selfless and honest.
Rather than using manipulation, or any of the other forms of deceit
that the world so often teaches us to use, godly leadership places
greater emphasis on what we can give rather than on what we can get.
I learned, yet again, that when we surrender to Jesus things change.
In saying "yes" to Him, He enters our lives, bringing with Him His
attitudes along with His way of living and working. Though many of
the leadership skills taught in our schools and business communities
are great, the core motivations that the world emphasizes have no
place in living the new life in Christ that we now have.

Having exposed my flawed motives, God continued to uproot
my paradigm of serving Him. In my time of recovery, I was made
aware that godly leadership, as a calling, goes way beyond the few
"superstar" leaders that I was trying to imitate. In fact, my search led
me to a place that I didn't expect. Reading my Bible, I found out that
leadership training begins in the home as we learn how to lead in our
family context.

The idea of learning leadership at home was a new idea for me. That
said, having been taught from the time I was a very small boy that,
as a man, I would be the spiritual leader of my home, I found that I
didn't really know what that meant. How was I going to get my wife
to follow my lead? What if she didn't want to follow? What if the
children got rebellious? With the questions and doubts came fear of
failure, failure as a husband, failure as a father, and failure as a family
leader. At the time, I had no idea that, if my wife knew that I loved
her, and if she experienced in me the kind of husband who laid down
his own self-interests to voluntarily serve her, she would gladly accept
my lead. She would do so because she trusted me and was confident
in my love for her, not because I demanded it of her as the head of
the home.

It turned out to be the same with the children. Some time ago, a parent asked me, "How do I get my children to do their chores? They are openly rebellious and I don't know what to do." The response given was, "They have to like you first. You can force obedience for a while, but people serve each other because they love each other." Godly parenting demonstrates love first and then teaches children out of that love, rather than simply demanding respect and enforcing obedience through various methods of punishment.

As I read about Jesus and His way of leading, I saw that even He refused to force relationships through controlling behavior. His kind of leadership was based on trust and love rather than on coercion and demand. Reminded of something my Grandpa said to me about leadership, I was taken back to a memory of a past conversation when Grandpa passed on some sage advice, "When you become a pastor, just remember that you're a shepherd, not a sheep dog."

Good image.

Jesus was a shepherd leader rather than a sheepdog leader. A man of action with a true shepherd's heart, bold and assertive, He was also totally non-self-centered. Jesus served and loved His sheep, giving His all for them by going to the cross as He sought to rescue them from their lostness. He loved them and they followed wherever He went, because they knew that He cared. In contrast to Jesus' style of spiritual leadership, a sheepdog leader can't wait long enough to build relationships based on trust with his followers. Using the tools of fear and coercion, he drives the sheep where he wants them to go, instead of taking time to love them and lead them.

As our model of godly leadership, Jesus came to proclaim a message rather than to build His ministry. Instead of gathering the "gifted" ones around Him, He gathered the foolish and the despised ones – a very mixed bag of people. He didn't demand performance, but gave mercy to all who would receive it from Him, transforming the hearts of those who surrendered to His love. He served those who followed Him as a Shepherd cares for his sheep. *Mark 10:45* records the words of Jesus as He taught His disciples about leadership:

> *"For even the Son of Man did not come to be served, but to serve, and to give His life a ransom for many."*

Jesus took time to teach his disciples what healthy leadership is and what it is not. With a strong emphasis on honesty and truthfulness, a godly leader is compassionate and seeks to bring redemption into the life of those whom he leads. A godly leader doesn't presume to force anyone to follow and yet provides a clear focus for those who choose to come after him. A godly leader takes the initiative. Seeing a need, he leads by moving to address the need rather than waiting for someone else to do so.

Action oriented, love based, and a servant by nature, a godly leader leads by example rather than by manipulation or coercion. He is merciful to imperfect followers and encourages them to continue the journey. People do things far beyond the norm for the love of a godly leader, giving loyalty of a depth that no one gives to a worldly leader. This is true in church. It is true in the workplace. It is true among friends. It is especially true in families.

Each of us is called to some element of leading, whether we see ourselves as being gifted that way or not. While it may be in a church, at home or at work, it will be in the context of some kind of relationship – a mother and her children, a husband and a wife, a businesswoman and her associates. That said, the leadership that we express as followers of Jesus is first found in laying down our privileges and equality, just as Jesus did, and in refusing to make our equality a priority to be held onto. Often our call to lead can be realized in laying down something that we could demand as our "right" and in taking the initiative to serve instead, doing what is most healthy by doing what is needed.

This is Jesus' kind of leadership. Calling us to learn from Him, He leads us in both learning to lead others and in learning how to choose the kind of godly leaders that we ourselves need to follow.

Pray: Come, Holy Spirit. I give this time to You, in Jesus' name.

Pray: Father in heaven, I give You the attitudes of my heart. I confess and renounce all that the world has taught me about leading that would orient me toward choosing a self-centered and manipulative life/relationship/ministry. Please bring to my mind anyone whom I have coerced or manipulated in the name of leading them.

(Take a moment and write down any names. This could be employees, children, parents, friends, or co-workers.)

Father, forgive me for manipulating ___________ in order to get my way.

Lord, I ask You to bring to my mind those who have manipulated me and whom I have held animosity against for the way that they have abused my trust.

(Take a moment and write down names.)

Forgive me for hating ___________/those in Your Church who have manipulated me and abused their power in doing so. I forgive them. Give me wisdom in such relationships, Lord, so I can have realistic expectations and can learn to set healthy boundaries. Jesus, I want to learn to lead from You by the power of Your Spirit. Open my eyes to the opportunities to lead in serving; help me to take the initiative. I put myself in Your hands for this purpose – that I might learn to serve as You did. I reject the lies of the Evil One and I set Your blood between him and me. Make me aware of his temptations to use self-centered and worldly leadership tactics. Always bring me back to You and to Your way of leading. I bless You and receive only what You give, in Jesus' name. Amen.

Day 13

The Name that is Above Every Name

"...He [Jesus] made himself nothing, taking the very nature of a servant, being made in human likeness. And being found in appearance as a man, he humbled himself by becoming obedient to death – even death on a cross! Therefore God exalted him to the highest place and gave him the name that is above every name, that at the name of Jesus every knee should bow, in heaven and on earth and under the earth, and every tongue acknowledge that Jesus Christ is Lord, to the glory of God the Father."

*Philippians 2:7-11 (**NIV**)*

In reading about how Jesus gave up His position and privileges in order to follow His calling, I found myself thinking about what kind of comparison might help us understand what He did.

 If He had been a senior citizen, He may have given up His right to a restful retirement after a hard life of work and struggle. If He had been a teen, He might have given up the opportunity to be popular and accepted among His peer group, where belonging is everything. If an athlete, it might have been the freedom of movement and physical abilities that are an athlete's greatest asset. If a young woman, it might have been the ability to have a child. If a young man, it might have been the opportunity to have a wife who would have been there to love Him through thick and thin. In whatever way that we measure it, Jesus paid a high cost when He gave up what was His in order to be obedient to His Father's will.

In contrast to who He had been in heaven before the creation of this world, He became a servant. A nothing.

He did so for you and for me.

Jesus had no illusions about the people He was coming to serve. He didn't come expecting to serve people who were noble and deserving. In coming to serve us in our childishness, our immaturity, our brokenness, and our self-centeredness, He didn't wait until we "got it together" or until we "cleaned up our act." He came to us in our places of deepest need and greatest selfishness. Knowing that because of our immaturity we would often abuse His grace in the process, He abandoned heaven and came to serve our needs.

Frequently He received no recognition. Many times He got no response. Often when there was a response it was a negative one, or worse, a half-hearted one. Yet the love of God must be expressed and that expression had to happen through a living, breathing person if it was to be real to those of us who needed it. So He came, and, when He came, He brought hope with Him.

The hope Christ brings is an amazing hope. It is the kind of hope that uproots both the power of past disappointment and the fear of future failure. It brings an assurance that something good is yet to come. We who receive it gain a sense that God is in control and that our future depends more on Him than on ourselves *(Romans 5:5-6)*.

In giving up His rights, Jesus placed Himself into the hands of the Father, depending on the Father for His identity. The Father responded to His act of faith by exalting Him and lifting Him up, giving Him the name that is above every other name, a name that will ultimately shake heaven and earth and bring all of creation to its knees.

A day is coming when we will stand with Christ Himself and be received into eternity with Him. Not all of earth, not any situation, not any enemy, not Satan himself, not all of the powers of hell can change that. We who lay our lives down now, and serve in the Spirit of Christ, will be known for all eternity as the sons and daughters of God. We will kneel in His presence, filled with joy as we utter His name, secure in the knowledge that we belong. Knowing the joy of

God in all its fullness, we will experience fully something that began in the moment of our first surrender to Him. Saved by Him, we will share in His glory for all eternity.

I am looking forward to that day!

Pray: Come, Holy Spirit. I give this time to You, in Jesus' name.

Pray: Father in heaven, I say "yes" to You and "yes" to Your call on my life. I want to obey you and lay my life down as Jesus did. I want to know what it means to serve You as He did, by the power of Your Holy Spirit. I want my identity to come from You. I want to be known in heaven as a servant of the Most High God and a child of the King of Kings.

To that end, I renounce my hold on this life. I renounce my demands that my life must go according to my plans rather than yours. Convict me, Lord, of what I am holding onto that I need to let go of. Show me the situations in my life where I am fearful of trusting You in the way that I need to trust You. Jesus, I renounce the identity that this life offers and I am ready to receive my identity from You. Come and rescue me from my fear of trusting You. I am at Your mercy.

(Take time here. Write down what comes to mind that you are holding onto and that you know stands between you and a fuller service to God. Pray and renounce it specifically).

I now renounce the lies of Satan that tempt me to live this life as though it were mine. Jesus, my life is Yours. As You open my eyes and empower me, I will walk more deeply in Your presence and in Your will. Let Your will be done in me. I bow before Your name even now and I anticipate the final day when I will bow with the rest of creation and proclaim Your Lordship.

I love You. In Your name, I pray. Amen.

Day 14

Continue to Work Out Your Salvation

"Therefore, my dear friends, as you have always obeyed – not only in my presence, but now much more in my absence – continue to work out your salvation with fear and trembling, for it is God who works in you to will and to act in order to fulfill his good purpose."

Philippians 2:12-13 (NIV)

The word "therefore" means "as a result."

As a result of knowing that Christ laid everything down in obedience to the Father's will, Paul encouraged the Philippian believers to obey God's will not just when he, Paul, was around to coach them, but as an everyday lifestyle; not because someone was looking over their shoulder, but as an expression of their love for Christ.

People who love someone act in that person's best interests because they want to rather than because they have to. Do we truly love Christ? If so, then we don't need anyone looking over our shoulder to make sure we live for Him. Our love for Him makes us want to give our all on His behalf.

Paul encouraged the believers, "Continue to work out your salvation." The word "continue" describes a relationship that has both a starting event and yet is ongoing. Using it, Paul speaks of salvation as an encounter with the Spirit of Jesus Christ that is meant to continue on into a lifelong relationship. In moving forward from the initial event into living in Christ, the reality of Jesus' gift to us is meant to percolate through, penetrating our whole lives with an awareness that gets increasingly real to us the more we live in it. Along with preparing us for eternity, salvation also encompasses all of life and every situation. Called to put our eternal souls in the hands of the Savior, Jesus, we are also called to live every moment of every day depending on His strength by the power of His Spirit.

The word "salvation" has an interesting synonym. It also means "deliverance."

Working out our salvation means learning to invite Jesus into every situation in which we find ourselves. It means living delivered from lostness and aloneness, knowing that our Savior is with us. As we increasingly call upon Jesus and learn to live in the Spirit's presence, we become increasingly able to sense His love for others and to experience the gratitude that this kind of freedom brings. Having been blessed by His presence, we begin to want others to experience what we have experienced.

Jesus did more than just save His disciples. He both lived with them and served them, though it has to be said that His service was different from the way we are often inclined to view "serving" someone. He certainly didn't park them on recliners somewhere and shower them with grapes and other dainties while they had their feet massaged.

Jesus took His disciples through real stretching as they had their self-centeredness stripped from them, so they could learn what Jesus wanted to teach them. Leading them into one situation after another in which they were helpless, He taught them to trust Him, situation by situation. Knowing the human tendency to rely on our own strength when we get into trouble, He also knew that the only way to teach reliance on God was to take His disciples into places where only the mercy and power of God could bring them through. As they practiced turning to Him for deliverance from whatever threatened to overwhelm them, He worked the message of His salvation and faithfulness through every aspect of their daily lives.

We can drift from God. How many of us remember when we first experienced the power of God? When we first knew His love closely? When we were active in sharing our faith? Maybe the passion for

Jesus and the sense of His presence that we once knew has gone, leaving us in a place where we just exist as we struggle to cope with the stresses of life. According to Galatians 5:1, we who begin with Christ in new freedom can sometimes wander back to the old slavery. If we find that the joy is gone and our walk with God seems heavy and draining, it could mean that we have wandered back to our old ways.

Paul tells us to fear this tendency to wander! To be aware! To tremble at the idea that, if we are not careful, neglect of our walk with God could lead to the loss of our intimacy with God. He encourages us to care for our relationship with Jesus and walk in it deliberately in order to keep from drifting back to the old ways in which we once lived. The same advice could be given to anyone who is in a long-term relationship. Taking seriously the importance of investing the time necessary to maintain and to continue to build our relationship with God will prevent us from waking up one day to find that we have drifted away and that our heart has gone cold toward Him. Many people, who have drifted in this way, wonder where the relationship they once had with God has gone and live with a sense of loss over it.

As we live in God's service, know this: it is God Himself who works in us to accomplish His will and His good purpose. As we live daily, situation to situation, in dependence on the Spirit of Jesus, He works in us. Even though dry times do come, as we walk with Him they also pass, so that we can once again know His presence and the freshness of His love just as we used to.

Pray: Come Holy Spirit. I give this time to You, in Jesus' name.

Pray: Jesus, save me from the illusion that I can live my faith without your involvement. Deliver me from self-dependence. Let me apply today, and everyday, the salvation that I have in You. Let that deliverance from self-strength be worked all the way through my life just like a baker works the yeast through the dough. Lord, I know my tendency to wander. I know my tendency to drift from you. Forgive me. I renounce my strength and place myself at Your mercy for Your power.

Father, I want to sense Your Spirit working in me to bring about

Your will. I want to look back at the end of each day and be able to see how You were with me. To that end, I renounce my will in order that Yours may be done. I give You the coldness and aloofness of my heart, so that I can be filled with Your passion to serve others in Your name and power. Come, Holy Spirit! I say "yes!" to You, in Jesus' name. Amen.

Day 15

You Shine Like Stars

"Do everything without grumbling or arguing, so that you may become blameless and pure, children of God without fault in a warped and crooked generation. Then you will shine among them like stars in the sky as you hold firmly to the word of life..."
Philippians 2:14-16 (NIV)

It is easy to let arguing and complaining take control of our lives. We may find it easy to argue with others, with God, and even with ourselves. The problem with complaining is that it takes our eyes off our Savior and puts them on our situation instead. In our negativity, often all we can see is what has gone wrong, and so we miss the blessing of being a part of what God wants to do with us in that moment.

As a college student, I had regular summer employment with the gas company in a large city. My job was fairly straightforward. I spent my days walking house to house and business to business reading meters, so that customers could be billed correctly for the gas they had used to heat their homes and places of employment. When I got the job, I had no idea it would be both boring and dangerous.

Long periods of boredom, punctuated by short bursts of adrenaline, were the norm as I walked from house to house, always on the watch but never knowing when I would be ambushed by a dog protecting its owner's property. It got so that I hated going to work and I spent my days living for quitting time. Grumbling from morning to night about the problems with my job, I was miffed that my summer was so boring. One day as I prayed that God would help me deal with the boredom and frustration, a strong, clear thought went through my mind, "Watch the people." As I processed what I sensed God was saying to me, it struck me that I had allowed myself to get caught up in grumbling over the negatives of the job. In seeing the days as something simply to be endured, I was losing out on the opportunity I had been given to connect with the people I encountered.

"Watch the people," the thought came again. Committing myself to the hands of God, I took action. Trusting that He would carry me through the days and give me the perspective I needed, I renounced my grumbling and began to watch the people, thanking God for where He had placed me.

That day everything changed. It was as though a whole new world opened up for me. No longer obsessed with simply getting through the days, I began to see the unique experiences I was being given. Opportunities came to be of help to people in need. One morning as I stood reading the meter in the basement of a house, I heard a crash upstairs. Bounding up the stairs three at a time, I found the eighty-five year old homeowner fallen and unable to get up. After carrying him to the couch and calling 911, I made sure he and his wife were taken care of before I left. It was only one of many experiences to follow.

The shift, from grumbling about my circumstance to praising God for where He had me, totally changed my perspective. Unable to be a blessing to anyone as long as my focus was on bellyaching about my situations, choosing thankfulness turned my focus to God and made me aware of opportunities to share with people that I had previously walked right by. Though I continued to deal with occasional dog attacks and disgruntled people, exchanging grumbling for thankfulness brought the joy back and made the days a challenge rather than drudgery.

Thankfulness can transform many less-than-ideal situations that we may find ourselves in. From struggling marriages to disappointing careers, keeping our focus on our Savior through thanksgiving allows us to rise above our circumstances and gives God the opportunity to use us where He has placed us. When we choose a grumbling lifestyle, not only do we sacrifice our witness, but we take on a manner that Christ has no part of. We miss out on the day that we are living in as we live for the change that we hope tomorrow will bring. Thankfulness allows us to make the most of what we have been given and to avoid living with regret over all we have missed.

Knowing the human tendency toward becoming negative as the challenges mount up, Paul kept calling the Philippians back to a lifestyle of thankfulness. Anyone can grumble and complain, because all of us have situations in our lives that are neither going well nor according to our plans. In choosing the way of thankfulness, our focus is drawn to our Savior. Regardless of where we find ourselves, we are kept in the awareness of who has us in that place. It is Christ Himself and he wants to use us where we are at.

I remember sitting in the ready-room one summer morning at the gas company, preparing to hit the streets with a dozen other meter readers. One of the guys, Benny, called out a generic greeting as he entered the room, "How goes it?!" Expletives filled the air around me, notable in terms of the negativity they expressed about how the fellows around me viewed their work. I chimed in with my contribution, too. "Great!" I yelled amidst the rumble of voices.

Benny jolted to a stop and spun on his heels to face me. Pointing his finger dramatically, he spoke, "I expect to hear that from you every time." Momentarily startled by the abruptness of his response, I asked him why. "Because you got God," he responded. I knew that Benny was aware of my faith in Christ, but I hadn't realized how intently he had been observing me as he sought to discover if my faith was more than just words.

Being a witness means reflecting the presence of Christ in whatever place, career, or situation we find ourselves, just as a light bulb's purpose is to provide light in whatever location the homeowner places it. Refusing to grumble, as we turn to Him in thanks, allows the Spirit of God to shine through us into the lives of those with whom He has placed us. He has put us where we are. He has a purpose in doing so. We don't have to worry that he might not use us, because being the people of His presence is what we were made for.

God has made us. He is our life. We can live rather than just exist. To those who say "yes" to Him, He gives family status. We belong. We can no longer be alone. Refusing to condemn us for our failings, He gives strength when our strength fails and others turn against us. When those we have depended on don't follow through, He calls our focus back to Himself. Giving us a grace that is always greater than the sin around us, He makes the truth about us plain – that our value to Him is so great that we are worth the life of Jesus given on the cross. From Him we receive blessing upon blessing. When life takes turns that are unexpected and costly to us, a thankful focus keeps us above our situation.

There is no place we can go where He will not follow us and find us. There is no situation that He cannot reclaim, if we will quit trying to fix it on our own and say "yes" to Him. In every place and situation in which we find ourselves, He calls us to look to Him and thank Him for His presence there. He has allowed us to be in those situations, so that we can learn surrender and trust. He will not leave us alone. Even if it was our own hard-headedness that got us into our difficult situation, He can and will redeem all that has happened.

Are we willing to thank Him in the midst of situations where we want to grumble instead? Are we ready to rejoice when things are difficult? Doing so gives Him opportunity to express His grace to us.

To *do all things without grumbling or disputing* (Philippians 2:14) is a call to give God His place as GOD in each stage of our lives, in each relationship that we have, in each struggle and disappointment that is ours.

It is an act of faith which says "Lord, I will rejoice that my situation is in Your hands. Deal with it as You will. I trust You!"

When we begin to live and "do" our lives with our focus on Him, we give God the opportunity to live and shine through us. Paul promises that, as we live this way, we can be sure that others will see His presence in us. Everything may not go smoothly, but, on a practical, day-to-day basis, we will be used by Him to shine His light into this world. We will be witnesses for Christ.

We are people in whom God's Spirit lives and through whom He makes His presence known. You are. I am. As we look to Him, the light of Christ shines through us into dark places and into the lives of hopeless people. It's why the Spirit of God calls us into the lives of others – to bring them hope.

Thy kingdom come, O Lord.

Sit back. Allow yourself to rest in God's presence.

Pray: Come, Holy Spirit. I give this time to You, in Jesus' name.

Pray: Father in heaven, forgive me for my complaining heart. Forgive me for arguing with You over why challenges are happening to me. Forgive me for soaking myself in self-pity and anger. I renounce this focus, in Jesus' name. I take my thoughts and the attitudes of my heart captive in Your name, Lord. I place my situation in Your hands. You are the Lord over every situation!

(Name the situation you have been complaining about.)

Jesus, my situation is now Yours. I am choosing to trust that You have it in Your hands right now, that You will walk me through it and bring something good out of it. I renounce the devil's work in my life through the difficult situations I have experienced and I command him to go to where You send him – out of my life forever! I thank You, Jesus, that I will see Your Kingdom come in my situation as You pour out Your Spirit on me. Come and fill me with Your Spirit.

Jesus, I now give the person/relationship ________________________________(name the person/relationship) I am struggling with into Your hands.

Jesus, he/she is now Yours. I place _________________ (name the person) into Your hands. I receive Your grace and strength. I receive Your truth. You will walk me through it. You will bring something good out of it. I release _______________ to Your blessing and I thank You that You are walking me through this to freedom. I renounce the devil's attempts to gain a foothold in my life through this broken relationship and I send that enemy away from me in Jesus' name! Lord, I will see Your Kingdom breaking into my life as You pour out Your Spirit on me. By the power of Your Spirit in me,

I am Your light in a dark world. Come and fill me continuously with Your Spirit, in Jesus' name. Amen.

Day 16

I Have No One Else Like Him

"I hope in the Lord Jesus to send Timothy to you soon, that I also may be cheered when I receive news about you. I have no one else like him, who will show genuine concern for your welfare. For everyone looks out for his own interests, not those of Jesus Christ. But you know that Timothy has proved himself, because as a son with his father he has served with me in the work of the gospel. I hope, therefore, to send him as soon as I see how things go with me. And I am confident in the Lord that I myself will come soon."

Philippians 2:19-24 (NIV)

One of the best ways to encourage others is to share the stories of how God's Spirit is moving. Not everyone is a gifted teacher, but most of us can tell a story.

In telling the stories of God moving among us, our testimonies bring much-needed encouragement to people who find themselves in trying circumstances. Our stories of God's faithfulness help men or women of God gain – and regain – the sense that they are not alone in proclaiming the message of Jesus. The stories of the Gospel having its effect are proof that the Spirit is bringing the kingdom of God to earth in life-transforming ways. We all periodically need to be encouraged in our service to God, to be reminded that God is effectively using us to bring a blessing to those in need of it.

Paul needed encouragement. Even while he was encouraging the

Philippians to look to God with thankfulness in everything, he himself was in danger of being overwhelmed by the immediate struggles that he was facing. He sent Timothy to bring back some stories from the Church at Philippi, so that he could be encouraged by the good things that were happening there.

Timothy was Paul's "proven" disciple. "Proven" means "tried" and "tested." Timothy had demonstrated that he was dependable and was committed to the journey regardless of what happened. Paul yearned for more "Timothys" who were willing to do what it took in order to carry the stories of encouragement to God's people.

People like Timothy are few. Mind you, few people have access to the kind of training that he had received. Timothy had lived with Paul through all of the Apostle's journeys and trials, gaining his training through situations that few of us ever experience. In trying to follow Christ, few of us do so with the kind of strength and commitment that Timothy had. A lifestyle like Timothy's comes with a cost, often requiring us to let go of the things that we have been trained to expect from life, in order to go and serve the Lord. Faced with that cost, many of us find ourselves backing away from our calling. Not Timothy. He threw everything aside and followed Paul into all kinds of situations for the sake of spreading the Gospel, making the hard choices necessary in order to do so.

Paul was no easy teacher to follow. He was a high-demand leader. In the manner of Jesus, Paul gave up everything for the sake of sharing the Gospel. He was a radical and anyone who followed him had to adopt the same lifestyle. Most people couldn't take the trials and challenges that the Apostle led them into. It was too much. They dropped out. Not that they lost their calling, it was just that they were unwilling to pay the cost in terms of self-surrender. Contemplating what it would take to partner with a minister of the Gospel like Paul, in the moment of turning their gaze from the heart of God, they lost sight of why they were doing what they were doing and quit (See *Acts 13:13; 2 Timothy 4:10*).

Timothy didn't quit. He held to his conviction that the place beside Paul was his to walk in. He kept his eyes on Jesus and let that focus lead him. By the power of the Holy Spirit, he engaged the lifestyle of a disciple. Having had his own heart captured by the heart of God, and knowing that the world was in danger of dying without hope, he couldn't shake the sense that his calling was to minister to that need.

Timothy carried a conviction that Jesus' compassion and the amazing news of his salvation had to be expressed to the whole world. Carrying a message of hope for the depressed and despairing, of freedom for the addicted and bound, of belonging for the lonely, of rescue for the lost, Timothy lived with a deep sense of the value that Jesus placed on the soul of each person that he came in contact with.

Timothy saw his purpose in terms of eternity. The touch of God on his life had been deep and had ruined him for the things of the world.

Have you ever felt that what you set your effort to was empty or short lived? Have you seen the end of a relationship even before it began? Do you look back on your career with a sense of fulfillment or has it been meaningless or a waste – "vanity" to use the words of the writer of Ecclesiastes?

Timothy was one of those who abandoned the priorities of his culture in order to bring the encouragement of Christ to those in need of it. Jesus' concerns became his concerns. Like Timothy, we need to be ruined for this world by the Gospel of grace as we allow Jesus' priorities to become ours. Each of us needs a mentor from whom we can learn and to whom we can offer our support, just as Timothy did with Paul. In offering ourselves to Christ as Timothy did, we surrender to the Holy Spirit as the one who strips us of our old motives and empowers us with His own.

Pray: Come Holy Spirit. I give this time to You, in Jesus' name.

Pray: Lord, I want to be a Timothy. Call me. Draw my focus to you. Forgive me for the times when I have held back from Your call. I know I cannot do it in my own strength, so I surrender myself to You. Uproot my shallowness of commitment. Deepen me. Train me. Give me mentors who are led by You. Let me experience the challenges that will form me as Your servant. "Prove" me as You "proved" Timothy. Let me be one who shares the stories and who encourages the servants of God who are in need. Jesus, I love You. I renounce the priorities and demands of this society in order to follow You wherever You take me, in Jesus' name. Amen.

Day 17

Finally, Rejoice!

"Finally, my brethren, rejoice in the Lord. To write the same things again is no trouble to me, and it is a safeguard for you. Beware of the dogs, beware of the evil workers, beware of the false circumcision; for we are the true circumcision, who worship in the Spirit of God and glory in Christ Jesus and put no confidence in the flesh..."

Philippians 3:1-3

Paul says, "Finally...rejoice in the Lord." He has written this to them before. But he does it again because he knows of the tendency that we all have to drift from the message of Jesus. The whole message of rejoicing in the life God has called us to is wrapped up in simply saying "yes" to the gift that is ours in Christ. Without conditions, other than our willingness to say "yes" to Him on an ongoing basis, we are accepted into relationship with Him. The heart of God, expressed to us in Jesus, yearns to demonstrate His love rather than just speak about it. Christ modeled for us a relationship with God that was more than living by a set of guidelines. We have been forgiven. Rather than waiting for us to seek Him out, He came looking for us, accepting us as we are and granting us mercy.

When Paul speaks of the followers of Christ as being the true circumcision, he is contrasting those who live by faith in Christ to a group that he refers to elsewhere in his other letters as the "circumcision party" *(Galatians 2:12)*. By emphasizing an attempt to please God through obedience to rules and religious ritual, the "circumcision party" that Paul is referring to is recognizable because of their need to add conditions to the grace that God gives so freely. Convinced that there is something that we have to do for God in order to make us feel that God's approval has been properly earned, they may try to make it a little harder for us to receive God's mercy by insisting that there is some kind of work, or penance, that has to be done in order to prove to God that we are worthy of eternal life.

Just as the circumcision party existed in Paul's day, there are religious groups today that carry many of the same characteristics. For some, it doesn't seem right that gaining a relationship with God should be so easy, so they set out to make it a little more difficult. Surely we have to do something to please Him, right? Paul emphatically says, "No!" The relationship with Jesus comes from an attitude of surrender and acceptance that is rooted in the human heart. It is a Holy Spirit-empowered response to God's call to us through Jesus. In some ways, it is beyond explanation. It can only be described as it has been experienced and can only be received as the Spirit of Jesus makes a person hungry for it.

People respond differently to the freedom and grace that Paul describes. Drawn to it, they see in the followers of Jesus something that they have yearned for and they come asking, "Help me find what you have."

Others hate the simplicity of it. Determined to get some credit for all the work they have put into their religion, they resist the idea of God's grace given as a free gift, wondering why the followers of Jesus should get something that they haven't had to work for. Why should people who have not done anything to please God be given peace, forgiveness, and freedom?

Paul tells us to be careful of people who come to us demanding that we look and act a certain way in order to please God, browbeating us with guilt and condemnation, telling us that God can't love us until we carry out whatever set of rules they tell us we must keep in order to please God.

To please God who says that there is now no condemnation for those in Christ – *Romans 8:1*.

To please God who says that He came to save and not to condemn – *John 3:17.*

To please God who sent angels to sing over the shepherds of the fields the message of *"peace among men with whom He is pleased."* Pleased enough to send Jesus to save them even before they knew how to surrender to His mercy *(Luke 2:14).*

To some the free gift is too good to be true and, if they cannot receive it, they will try to prevent others from doing so as well. Believing that God is too holy to accept just anyone, the group that Paul warns us about imposes laws and performance requirements that we must carry out in order to prove how sorry we really are. They either forget or just don't understand that the Spirit of God sees what is in our hearts well before we can do anything on the outside to prove it.

In his urgency to warn us of the dangers of the circumcision party, Paul graphically compares them to a pack of dogs. Demanding perfect religious performance, they use guilt tactics, put conditions on God's love, and run other people down, killing faith just like a pack of feral dogs will harass, pursue, and kill a farmer's livestock. Paul warns that such people are dangerous to the freedom that we have been given to simply trust God and to receive the freedom He offers through Christ.

Don't listen to anyone who tells you that you have to do something to please God. Say "yes" to His love. Don't let go of that "yes" no matter how badly you stumble. He will never leave you. He cannot be unfaithful to love you. Where your sin is overwhelming, His grace is greater than your sin *(Romans 5:20).* God won't give up on you even if you don't look like you deserve it.

Sometimes in the midst of our stumbling, with the dogs of condemnation and conditional love nipping at our heels, it is difficult to keep this focus. That is why Paul repeats it. His repetition is an encouragement to lean into our call to keep our eyes on the Savior. So he says, *"Rejoice, and again I will say it, rejoice!" Be joyful! Be thankful! Praise Him!*

Pray: Come, Holy Spirit. I give this time to You, in Jesus' name.

Pray: Jesus, I am Yours. Open my eyes to those in my life that seek to load up my worship of you with rules and conditions. When people try to kill my faith with guilt and condemnation, remind me that my faulty performance has nothing to do with Your love for me. I accept the gift of Your love for me unconditionally. I give You all my sin. I renounce all of the practices that would make my faith into a false, performing type of religion. I am in Your hands as a child of God who has said "yes" to Jesus. Standing in Your grace, and dependent on Your strength, I desire to run the race You have set before me. Believing that You knew what You were doing when You called me, I rejoice in the calling You have given me, in Jesus' name. Amen.

Day 18

Rubbish!

"...for we are the true circumcision, who worship in the Spirit of God and glory in Christ Jesus and put no confidence in the flesh..."

Philippians 3:3

The "true circumcision" refers to those who have God's mark on their hearts, rather than on their outward flesh. We who trust God belong to Him. Looking to the motives of our hearts rather than the outward skills or status that we possess, it doesn't matter to Him what we look or sound like. Whether a businessman in a suit or a street person in ripped jeans, whether a top athlete or living with the physical challenges of cerebral palsy and scoliosis as my brother did, whether we come from a well-put-together religious family or find ourselves living in the aftermath of a failed relationship, who we are on the outside doesn't affect God's love for us. In any heart that will make room for Him, He comes. The rejoicing and hope that He creates in our lives mark us as His.

I didn't always understand that God cares less for my religious qualifications than he cares for my heart. Neither did Paul. Living with a mentality that placed value on the ability to perform well religiously, Paul spent years striving to please God only to realize after he came to faith in Christ that all his qualifications meant nothing in comparison to having a heart filled with love for God.

"...although I myself might have confidence even in the flesh. If anyone else has a mind to put confidence in the flesh, I far more:

If outward appearances and qualifications could please God, he had more than enough to do the job. Paul was well trained and highly skilled. A religious over-achiever and at the top of his class, he was brilliant, an expert of experts.

Paul's religious qualifications weren't enough to bring the peace he sought. Somewhere within him, he knew that his accomplishments couldn't buy God's favor and his lack of fulfillment just made him angry and driven.

Encountering Jesus altered the way Paul viewed his achievements. His experience of the mercy of God on the road to Damascus changed him. Things once important to him suddenly held little value. The things from which he had once gained his sense of identity had become meaningless. Having gained a new identity and purpose, one freely given and freely received, he recognized that his attempts to honor God by his performance had actually held him back from truly experiencing the Love of God. Choosing the worship of the heart that came by faith rather than by performance, he let go of his old striving. Along with it went the guilt, the anger, and the hopelessness that came from not being able to measure up, no matter what he did.

The changes that came about in Paul's life, as a result of coming to know the love of God, happen in anyone who truly falls in love. Altering how we see ourselves and what we value, being loved unconditionally causes our priorities to shift radically. All of the things we once poured our lives into, built up, or hoarded over the years don't matter anymore. To someone truly in love, the only thing that matters is to be in the presence of the one we love and who loves us back. When we are with someone like that, we begin to experience what it means to no longer have to perform in order to receive approval. We come to realize that we are loved, not for what we do, but for who we are. Undeserved love is so incredibly impacting that it can even help us love ourselves, because it gives us a new perspective on our value through the eyes of the one who loves us.

All the rest, by contrast, seems like garbage. Paul describes his own experience vividly:

> *"But whatever things were gain to me, those things I have counted as loss for the sake of Christ. More than that, I count all things to be loss in view of the surpassing value of knowing Christ Jesus my Lord, for whom I have suffered the loss of all things, and count them but rubbish so that I may gain Christ..."*
> Philippians 3:7-8

Speaking of the emptiness of his previous accomplishments and the misplaced sense of identity he tried to get from them, Paul describes his past efforts to please God as though they actually made him unhealthy rather than making him a better person. Painting the picture of someone who has been hugging and cradling armfuls of rancid, worm-ridden garbage, nuzzling his face into it, crooning over it as though in love with it, he describes someone who is poisoning himself by the very rottenness of what he holds so close. Worse yet, the garbage is all he knows, and his whole purpose in life is to get more of the same.

Suddenly a gift of clean, delicious food is offered to this person. Having sampled it, the contrast with what he is used to is so dramatic that the person rejects the old garbage with force and totality. Once he has seen and tasted the healthy food, there is no comparison to be made. Taking no time to sort through the old garbage to see what might be kept, he throws it from himself with vehemence!

The rotten garbage in the above picture represents the performance-based way of relating to God that so many "religious" folk have been trained in. The clean, delicious food is the life of grace that Christ calls us to and which He freely gives to those who are willing to receive it. Being two very different realities, once you have tasted one, attempting to live in the other becomes repugnant. Paul says that the life lived in the love of God is so far above what he grew up in that to compare the two is ridiculous. The old way is like rancid garbage. The new life is worth trading everything for.

All that said, there are times in which we are tempted to try to bring some of our old way of living back into the new life we have been given by Christ. Sorting through our old qualifications in order to see what we have to offer God, our pride can tempt us to think that we did accomplish something after all. Whispering in our ear, the devil tells us that we had better be careful not to throw it all away!

Not so with Paul. He claims that if we have really come to know what we have received in Christ, it makes us so desire to be with Him that we lump all of our past accomplishments together and chuck them in the trash.

All of our old accomplishments are filthy, rancid garbage in comparison with the gift of life in Jesus. We need to be aware that the things that the world will praise us for are toxic to our spiritual health, causing pride to form in us and splitting our allegiance between worldly things and Christ Himself. Paul said that there can only be one top priority for us. He desired only that he might be...

> *"...found in Him, not having a righteousness of my own derived from the Law, but that which is through faith in Christ, the righteousness which comes from God on the basis of faith..."*
>
> *Philippians 3:9*

As we say "yes" to Jesus, the Holy Spirit strips away our guilt along with the frustration of failed performance. Giving a new sense of identity and purpose, He makes us free to enter the believer's rest *(Hebrews 4:1-2)*.

Pray: Come, Holy Spirit. I give this time to You, in Jesus' name.

Pray: Above all else, Lord, let me be found in You. Let me be found free from non-stop striving. Let me be found free from finding my identity in my successes and failings. Let me be found free from the nagging worry of not being able to measure up, from the fear that I will be seen as I am, and from the worry that I may bring disgrace to You. Let me live in freedom from condemnation, self-hatred, and disappointment over not having made the impact for You that I think I should have. Allow me to live in the joy of knowing and understanding that You are glad to see me and to be with me because of who I am rather than what I do. Lord, I bless You. I abandon the old life. Everything that I have seen as an asset I give to You. Everything I have held back, because I saw it as a liability, I give to You. Use me, in Jesus' name. Amen.

Day 19

Clear the Way!

"'Comfort, O comfort My people,' says your God.
'Speak kindly to Jerusalem;
And call out to her, that her warfare has ended,
That her iniquity has been removed,
That she has received of the LORD's hand
Double for all her sins.'"

Isaiah 40:1-2

God comes, by the power of His Spirit, with a message of comfort declaring that we no longer have to fight our guilt and the condemnation that comes with it. Because of Christ, that battle is over.

Proclaiming that Jesus accomplished peace between God and ourselves at the cross *(Colossians 1:20),* the Apostle Paul taught that God is not angry at us. Rather than condemning us, the Spirit of Christ Jesus calls us into the living reality of His peace, introducing us to our compassionate Heavenly Father who is determined to lift our judgment from us.

The words of Isaiah remind us of Jesus' words in *John 14:16.* Saying that He will send the Holy Spirit to be our "Comforter" and our "Helper", He promises to be the help we need.

The Spirit helps us in ways far deeper than simply ignoring our brokenness and telling us that "it's all okay." Rather than avoiding our flaws, He exposes them out of concern for our well-being. Laying bare what is unhealthy in the way we are living, He does so in order that He may help us where we need it most – in the place where our sense of guilt and failure drags us down (See *Psalm 139:23-24*). Comforting the weary, He assists the downhearted. In the moment of exposing our weaknesses, He calls us into deeper relationship with Christ. He comes to help, knowing that, on our own, we are lost.

The Holy Spirit is also known as the "One Who Comes Alongside." The Greek word translated "comforter/helper" is the same word used to describe how a larger ship would come alongside a smaller ship in a storm. As the larger ship came alongside, it would block the wind and create a calm place, a "lee," for the smaller ship to sail in. In this way, it could both shelter and help the smaller ship into port – saving the smaller ship from certain destruction.

In the movie, "Perfect Storm," there is a scene where the captain of a coast guard cutter places his ship upwind of drowning airmen. In the lee of the ship, his rescue crew risks their own lives in order to save those who would otherwise die. This captain was a comforter and a helper. He was truly "one who comes alongside."

 Coming alongside is what God is speaking of through Isaiah when He says: *"Comfort My people,"* foretelling the promise of Jesus who would ultimately send His Holy Spirit upon us. In Jesus' gift of the cross, He removed our sin, paid our price, and declared that we are His. We belong. Punishment is no more because Jesus took our punishment on Himself. In receiving the gift of forgiveness that He offers, we can find the rest we need and the security of knowing that we are loved by God.

As in any relationship, God seeks a response from those He has reached out to.

> *"A voice is calling,*
> > *'Clear the way for the LORD in the wilderness;*
> > *Make smooth in the desert a highway for our God.*
> *Let every valley be lifted up,*
> > *And every mountain and hill be made low;*
> > *And let the rough ground become a plain,*

Speaking of the hidden and lonely places within us, the places where we hide from God as we struggle to cope with our weaknesses in isolation, Isaiah describes the human heart as a wilderness, empty of God's presence.

Isaiah pictures the wilderness of the heart as a place difficult to negotiate. Filled with rough terrain representing the things that block us from seeing God and the grace He offers to us, we carry hurts, offenses and failures. Living with self-hatred, betrayal, and disappointment, we struggle with anger, un-met needs, control issues, and demonic influences. Giving new meaning to the term "in over your head", such things become high mountains and deep valleys for us, easy to get lost in and difficult to find a way out of. It's tough to see over the hills when you are stuck at the bottom of a valley.

The Spirit of God calls us to "prepare a way." Calling us to say "yes" to His request, He asks that we turn toward Him on a heart level. As we respond to His love and calling, God Himself lifts us from the valleys of betrayal and broken relationships. Revealing to us that there is more to living than our experiences would lead us to believe, our "yes" gives God's Spirit the opportunity He needs to clear the obstacles from our lives as He leads us into the journey of freedom and meaning that we were originally created for.

Having issued a call, this passage comes with a promise as well, declaring that as we make a way for God in our hearts...

> *"...the glory of the LORD will be revealed,*
> *And all flesh will see it together..."*

Isaiah 40:5

We will see God! In fact, the Bible teaches us that, in Christ, we already have! *(John 14:9)*. All of the glory of God is poured out on us in the person of Jesus *(Philippians 2:6)*. All the compassion of God, all the hope he gives, all His love and grace, shine on us in the face of the risen Christ. Our present situations will not have the last say - not the pain of divorce, the betrayal of a rebellious child, the oppressing power of drug addiction, or the betrayal of a friend. None of these things will have the last say. Both the prophet Isaiah and John the Baptist called out:

 "Clear a way for the LORD!"

Christ will have the last say! His final word will be a glorious expression of His goodness and mercy to all of us who are willing to receive.

Pray: Come, Holy Spirit. I give this time to You, in Jesus' name.

Pray: Dear Jesus, I clear a way in the wilderness of my heart and mind for You to come to me. I ask You to show me all that would block me from knowing You and everything that could keep me from surrendering my life and heart to You. Uproot it all and bring me to freedom. I give You ________________________________ _______.

(List anything that holds you back, and speak it to God. "My anger... My bitterness...My failure...My inability to trust after what was done to me...My depression over...").

Dear Lord Jesus, Lord Holy Spirit, I give You my mountains and my valleys. I renounce them. I am ready for You to level them and to show me Your glory. Today I lay down my struggle to make my way in this world. I give You my striving. I cast myself on Your mercy. I renounce the demonic powers that have tried to deceive me and I give myself into Your hands.

Thank You, Jesus, that I am beloved. Thank you for the worth that I have in Your eyes. Thank You that You did not demand that I come to You first, but that You came to me. Even now, Lord, as You come to me, I ask You to penetrate my wilderness and bring me into Your life. I am Yours. Of all that comes to me, I accept only what comes through Your hand. I trust that in Your compassion You will be my protector, in Jesus' name. Amen.

Day 20

That I May Know Him and the Power of His Resurrection

"More than that, I count all things to be loss in view of the surpassing value of knowing Christ Jesus my Lord, for whom I have suffered the loss of all things, and count them but rubbish so that I may gain Christ, and may be found in Him, not having a righteousness of my own derived from the Law, but that which is through faith in Christ, the righteousness which comes from God on the basis of faith, that I may know Him and the power of His resurrection and the fellowship of His sufferings, being conformed to His death; in order that I may attain to the resurrection from the dead."

Philippians 3:8-11

The old saying that we can't have the best of both worlds is one that the Apostle Paul would agree with. He says we have to trade one world for the other. We often struggle to follow Jesus because we fail to grasp Christ's call to lose this world in order to gain the next.

Paul's words to the Philippians mirror Jesus' teaching that, in order to follow Him, we must lose the lifestyle that our society teaches us to expect in this world. With six repetitions *(Matthew 10:39; 16:25; Mark 8:35; Luke 9:24; 17:33; John 12:25),* the Gospel writers emphasized strongly the high degree of importance that Jesus placed on His followers taking this to heart.

For the person ready to take seriously the call to abandon living by this world's standards, Jesus promises that he will not walk in darkness but will have the "Light of life" *(John 8:12)*.

Many of us who have committed to follow Christ, at some point in our lives, have failed often enough that we finally come to the point of giving up on our sense of calling. Having sinned the same sin so often that we can no longer bring ourselves to ask for forgiveness, we live in guilt and fear, angry at ourselves for our failure. Remaining true to His calling on our lives, God draws us to a moment of choice. Will we choose our old familiar way of dealing with the struggle or will we surrender to the call, and way, of the Holy Spirit? In making the choice to cease trying to earn God's love and approval by the way we fight our temptation, surrendering to His grace means opting for His way and resources rather than our own.

Understanding that we couldn't quit sinning on our own, Christ came to give Himself on our behalf. He came so that we could quit fighting our sin and just give Him our sin instead. He came to offer us His love regardless of what we have done or how many times we have done it. The hope that becomes ours in allowing Him to do in our lives what He came to do is what the "Light of life" refers to. Called to place ourselves into His hands, along with our weaknesses and our sins, God seeks to convince us that He will love us even if we can't fix ourselves. It means being able to stop trying to clean up our act and learning to just give our act to Him.

Jesus would never say that it is okay to sin, or that this life will be easy or a smooth ride. What He did teach is that we will get a lot further in breaking free of sins, such as lust, greed, envy, pride, etc., if we depend on God's help, rather than merely trying to "reform" our behavior through our own willpower and resolutions. We don't need reformed hearts. We need transformed hearts – something only God can give us. Christ doesn't ask us to prop up His reputation. He calls us to be His witnesses. In carrying God's presence, instead of His reputation, freedom becomes our "normal", while carrying the old ongoing sense of guilt becomes abnormal.

We need to pray prayers like this: "Dear Jesus, I am done trying to impress You by performing for You. I am done living in fear that I might fail you and make you angry with me. Forgive me for not trusting that You love me. I give You both my sin and all my futile efforts to stop sinning. I realize that I have been trusting myself instead of You. I renounce that self-trust and surrender to You in order to trust You for all things. Let me live in the reality of Your love for me. I accept Your righteousness in me. In Your name I ask. Amen"

Those are risky prayers because, as we pray prayers like that, we are saying that we are ready to lose our lives in order to live His life. In order to live in a world that is hostile to God, we must understand that we will experience some of the hostility that Jesus experienced simply because we represent someone the world hates. Our experience of life and ministry will be joined to His experience and God will show us some of what He went through in order to allow us to understand the extreme nature of His love for us and for those around us. We will suffer at times, but in the place of suffering we will know a strength that is not ours and that we cannot experience unless we step out of our own lives and into His.

Paul calls it knowing "the power of His resurrection and the fellowship of His sufferings."

The Bible teaches that the same Spirit who raised Jesus from the grave lives in us who believe. Coming to live in us, the Holy Spirit manifests His power in our weakness *(2 Corinthians 12:9)*. In giving our weaknesses to God, rather than spending our lives fighting them, we experience the power of God as He pours his strength into our lack.

If God is to make a real difference in our lives, He has to become more than just a concept to us. Received by faith, God becomes a concrete and real presence, demonstrating Himself in our lives as we live here where He has placed us. Dependent on His power for everyday living, in every situation in which we find ourselves, we say, *"Come, Lord Jesus! Come, Holy Spirit!"*

Pray: Come, Holy Spirit. I give this time to You, in Jesus' name.

Pray: Dear Lord Jesus, as Paul says in the passage above, let me be conformed to Your death. Just as a dead person lets go of everything that the previous life held, I want to let go of the twisted priorities of my old life. What used to matter no longer matters. What used to be important no longer is. I want to let go of all of the striving to manage my life for my own purposes and, as an eternal person, I want to begin to live in the freedom that such change brings.

Lord, I now let go of everything that I have been hanging onto. I am Yours. Show me what You want of me. Come, Holy Spirit. I am ready to place it all before You.

Take a moment of quiet to ask yourself a couple of questions.

What do you spend the most amount of time worrying about? Write it out. Living with this kind of worry often means you are struggling in your own abilities, not really trusting God to be your strength. Write out what comes to mind.

What is the event that you go back to that has been a source of fear for you? Write it out. Living with this kind of fear often means you are coping with your woundedness by your own resources rather than allowing Him the access He needs in order to heal you. Write out what comes to mind.

Say, "Jesus, come into the memory of this event." Physically hold your hands out to Him and drop the situation/memory into His hands.

Say, "Jesus, I let it go. I am ready to enter "the fellowship of Your sufferings." I trust that, when you allow me to experience some of the sufferings that you went through, You will not give me more than I can bear. I am ready to trust that You will be my strength in all that I experience. I reject everything that comes from the devil and ask that You lead me. In my weakness, Your strength is made perfect.

Jesus, I invite Your Spirit and Your power into the suffering that I have experienced. Open my eyes to see Your presence all around me. I abandon my strength in order to trust You and Your strength in me.

Conform me to Your death, Jesus. By the power of the Holy Spirit, who raised You from the dead, I renounce the cares of this world that I have written above. I renounce the power of my own strength, a strength that has always failed me. I bind and reject the powers of the devil, whose strength is so much greater than mine but which is absolutely nonexistent compared to Your strength working through me. I accept that I died to the old self when I gave myself to You. I accept the new life You give and the freedom to begin to live above my circumstances as You pour your Spirit around me and through me.

Jesus, I know that I was made for eternity and that I will be fully raised from the dead on the last day to be with You in heaven. I love You and anticipate that day. Until then, let me live in You and I ask You to live through me, in Jesus' name. Amen!

Day 21

Forgetting What Lies Behind

"...in order that I may attain to the resurrection from the dead. Not that I have already obtained it or have already become perfect, but I press on so that I may lay hold of that for which also I was laid hold of by Christ Jesus. Brethren, I do not regard myself as having laid hold of it yet; but one thing I do: forgetting what lies behind and reaching forward to what lies ahead, I press on toward the goal for the prize of the upward call of God in Christ Jesus."

Philippians 3:11-14

Anticipation and the excitement it brings creates hope.

I am not in heaven yet, and neither are you if you are reading this, but I will be. The thought that we will be there together excites me.

This is hope in action. Hope brought by Jesus, who has laid hold of me, brings excitement for the future. I know that there is more to come and that what will come is good!

It's like getting engaged.

The day I asked my wife to marry me, I went into action. I booked the church. I booked the hall. I booked the photographer and the cars and the tuxes and... well, you get the picture.

She had said "yes," and I believed her. She loved me and her love had "laid hold" of me. When she said "yes" to my proposal, I believed her so much that I started spending my money in an uncharacteristic way. In a sense, though, I was not yet married; it was as though the promise of being married had become so certain to me that I was already acting as if it was a done deal. Though the actual event was still out in front of me, I wanted it to hurry and arrive, so that I could leave bachelorhood behind! To that end, I focused my daily living.

A friend of mine experienced this kind of excitement over a future hope in a different way as she booked the trip of a lifetime. Being single at the time, she didn't relate to the marriage thing, but she had wanted to take a year and travel the world. Buying a ticket headed west, she planned to go in that direction until she arrived back home again. In anticipation, she began to make preparations. Work schedules changed. Money was put away. Immunizations were brought up to date. Visits with friends that she wouldn't see for a year became a regular thing, and the topic of conversation always turned to the adventure that lay ahead. Even though the trip was months away, she had already begun and the excitement was contagious, making even her day-to-day drudgery at work easier to live with. Hope had "laid hold" of her!

Another friend had spent decades in a dead-end job. The dream of retirement was so far away that it had become almost a thing of despair. Waiting for it to come, he felt as though he was just existing. How much longer? Trying to avoid thinking about it, because he couldn't stand how long he had to wait, he hated his work and the sense of being trapped in it. He had bills, the pay was good, and he couldn't get out. How much longer would it be? Suddenly the day came! Retirement was upon him! The years had gone by and it was soon! That realization changed him and he began to live what he was not yet fully experiencing. Some kind of hope had "laid hold" of him!

Living in Jesus is sort of like living in two worlds at once. There is the promise of a future that is so powerful that it invades the now, taking over the thought life, and changing the behavior of those affected by it. Bringing about hope and an anticipation that is exciting, as we look forward to what God has for us, it causes us to want to let go and gives us a desire to move ahead. Trying to describe it is always a struggle, because our illustrations fall short, speaking only of what we plan, unable to convey what God plans.

Whatever we plan always has an element of uncertainty to it, but whatever God plans is certain, and Paul says that God has planned our future. Jesus has "laid hold" of us with the intent of bringing us into eternal life. Just as a lifeguard "lays hold" of a drowning person with the intent of saving him, Paul says that God has more for us than this life can bring us. God has made our future certain. An earthly bride can get cold feet. Travel plans can fail. A financial crash can ruin the best-laid retirement plans.

But God cannot fail us!

In the reality of our day-to-day living, we can often lose focus on our future with God, but God never loses His focus on His future plans for us. Seeking us out wherever we are, He calls us, drawing us into relationship with Himself. When we stumble, He is there to pick us up. When we lose our focus, He calls us back to His love for us. Having laid hold of us, He is faithful to carry us forward on the journey.

Paul teaches that life in Christ is like a trip. Once we say "yes" to Jesus, passage to heaven is booked and we are on the way. The journey has begun and, though it can be a bit frustrating, because we still have to live in this world for a while and do what needs to be done here, God cannot be unfaithful to His promise to get us there. For those of us who look forward to eternity with Christ, the farther we find ourselves on the journey, the more this world begins to pale in comparison with what lies ahead.

Led by the Spirit of Christ, we gain hope for the future. Not knowing what the future holds, we know who holds the future. Knowing who holds the future, and that He is faithful even when we fail to be, the hope He gives strips the fear of disappointment away, allowing us to live in joyful anticipation *(Romans 5:5)*.

If He has laid hold of you, He will take you there. Live here as though you have let go of what is past and have laid hold of what is coming. Live like heaven is yours. Live like you belong, because you do. I do, too. The past is past and the future belongs to the children of God.

If you still carry the past, it's time to give it to Jesus. It is time to stop letting what is ahead of you be dictated by what happened behind you. Let it be done. Let His blood wash it away. Set your eyes on God who calls you. Heaven awaits and there are adventures to be lived between now and then.

Pray: Come, Holy Spirit. I give this time to You, in Jesus' name.

Pray: Jesus, I am Yours. Thank You for Your promises to me. Thank You for Your call on my life and for Your love for me. I accept that You have called me and that I am now Your child. I accept that heaven awaits me and that You, having called me, will bring me there. Jesus, I give You all that lies behind me. Lord, show me anything that needs to be resolved, and reveal to me what needs to be done in order to resolve it. I am ready to obey. It is all Yours. I put it all under Your blood and accept my freedom and the hope that You bring me.

Satan, the Lord rebukes you! My past is under Jesus' blood and I have given it to Him. I now understand that it is gone and that you cannot hold me back from following Jesus. In Jesus' name I command you to go where He sends you. Leave me now! As I stand under His protection, I place the blood of Jesus between me and you.

Dear Lord, I look forward to living in Your presence and I receive the upward call that You have on my life. I trust that You, in Your faithfulness, will take me there, in Jesus' name. Amen!

Day 22

I Press on Toward the Goal!

"I press on toward the goal for the prize of the upward call of God in Christ Jesus."

Philippians 3:14

We are called to press on toward the same goal as the Apostle Paul.

The goal is not heaven. The goal is a life of surrender to Christ.

The prize is heaven - an eternity with God.

Those crossing the goal line will receive the prize.

A life lived fully in surrender to Jesus Christ. Called to press toward that goal, none of us is fully there yet. Whether we speak of living in surrender to the Spirit of Jesus, or of belonging to the body of Christ, both are ways of saying that we are a part of the family of God. As children of the Heavenly Father, we are those in whom the Spirit of God cries out, *"Abba! Father!" (Galatians 4:6).*

As we come to understand that living a surrendered life is not something that we can do by our own initiative or personal power, the Holy Spirit both calls and empowers us to increasingly abandon our own strength in order to live in Christ's strength. With the Spirit of God having the freedom to use us as He wills, it is up to God to make sure that our lives are used in a meaningful way. It's what Jesus meant when He told His disciples to Pray: "Thy Kingdom come and

Thy will be done…in my life as it is in heaven!" (My paraphrase).

God wants to use us for more than we can imagine or desire. Surrendering everything to Him means giving Him the freedom to use us in any way, and in any place, that He chooses. As surrender to Him becomes our daily reality, we gain a new focus for our living as our lives become increasingly more about His power and authority working through us – "Thy Kingdom come," not mine. His purposes begin to become our desires as we pray, "Thy will be done," not mine.

Surrender to God can't be accomplished through motivational preaching or personal effort. Having tried, I didn't do well. Struggling to make my life live up to the ideal that I so often preached, I finally came to the end of myself. Becoming angry and disillusioned with following God, I also became depressed. Ready to give it all up and be done, it was then that I began to learn about the difference between performing for God and living in surrender to God.

According to Paul, in order to move forward, we have to let go of what lies behind. With a tendency to want to live in our own way and strength that is as strong as our survival instinct, surrendering to God requires becoming fed up with what holds us back. Unable to get there on our own, we are dependent on God to bring us to that point *(John 6:44)*. Knowing that our inherent selfishness fights the process of surrendering to Him, the Lord doesn't leave our following Him up to human effort. Sending His Spirit to guide us through to the place of surrender, He allows frustration to creep in and disillusionment with this life to build as a part of that journey. Watching our plans for life fragment and come apart prepares us to be done with the old way of life while making us ready for change in the same way that watching our old car fall apart piece by piece makes us ready to commit to the purchase of a new one.

Jesus emphasizes God's role in "drawing" us *(John 6:44)*. No one can come to Him unless the Father draws that person. Not a pastor. Not a church elder. Not a nice person. Not a desperate person. No one! God Himself opens our eyes to His calling on our lives.

To the person who doesn't know Jesus, the Spirit of God reveals the Savior and draws him to surrender his eternal destiny into the hands of God.

To the new Christian who has no idea how to live in surrender to Jesus, the Spirit of Christ joins her to other believers who can help her learn.

To the Christian who believes in God, but who has wandered from his relationship with Jesus and is no longer serving Him, the Spirit of God draws him back to his first love - back to giving it all over to Jesus.

In the case of the betrayed person who has been burned so many times that she cannot trust anymore, the Spirit draws her to once again trust Him whom the scripture describes as "faithful" *(1 Corinthians 1:9)*.

Before we really understand the damage we do to ourselves in our tendency to wander away from God, many of us spend the first part of our relationship with God yo-yoing back and forth, first walking closely with Christ and then wandering away, until something radical happens to bring us to a point of real surrender.

Refusing to quit drawing us back, the Spirit of God teaches us that this life of surrender is more than a one-time thing. To someone who has experienced his attempts to follow Jesus running dry over and over again, this is wonderful news. Realizing that we need help to walk with Jesus, we learn to press into God even as He presses into us. Our desire shifts from getting God to fix our situation to just having God keep us close. Surrender to Him means saying "yes" to the one who can cause us to stand in the Savior's presence on a daily basis *(Jude 24)*.

In letting go of what has been in our past and pressing forward to the goal, we will receive the prize – the high and upward call of God in Christ Jesus. Heaven will be our eternal home.

Pray: Come, Holy Spirit. I give this time to You, in Jesus' name.

Pray: Dear Jesus, in my heart I want to follow You. I want to press forward to the goal. Lord, I now know that I have a calling and that I need to live in the surrender that You are calling me to. Forgive me for the times when I have lived for the prize rather than for the relationship with You. I know that living for You is not just about getting to heaven but about becoming Yours so that Your Spirit can live through me here and now.

Jesus, I want my life to be Yours. I surrender myself into Your hands. I ask You to draw me deeper. I ask You to reveal more of Yourself to me. Show me when I am striving to live for You in my own strength. Draw me to that place in my life where I am willing to surrender all to You. Take me there step by step. I know it doesn't happen all at once but that it is a process that You lead me through day by day. Continue this process of surrender in me. I lay down my striving this very moment. Take me. Call me. Draw me. All that You have promised to bring to bear in my life, I say, "Let it be done." I am Yours, in Jesus' name. Amen.

Day 23

All of Us Who Are Perfect

"I press on toward the goal for the prize of the upward call of God in Christ Jesus.
Let us therefore, as many as are perfect, have this attitude; and if in anything you have a different attitude, God will reveal that also to you; however, let us keep living by that same standard to which we have attained."

Philippians 3:14-16

Paul is speaking to those of us who are perfect. Perfect means "pure" and "holy."

A "perfect" person is a forgiven person; a person who has had their impurities wiped away by the blood of Christ.

An imperfect person is one who holds onto his guilt, failing repeatedly as he tries to compensate for His own sins by being a "good" person, rather than receiving the forgiveness that Jesus offers.

Romans 3:21-24 says that God has revealed His righteousness in Christ. It is the holiness of God and is given as a gift to those who simply believe, trust, and receive it from Him.

Some of us live with our guilt everyday. We know how sinful we are. How could we ever be seen as being "perfect" before God? No one is perfect before God!

Paul is trying to communicate as strongly as he can that we are God's chosen and beloved children. We are not just stinking sinners that

God has chosen to put up with as we stumble along making a mess of life. Unable to cleanse ourselves of our guilt, Christ has done it for us. Jesus' gift of righteousness, through the shedding of His blood for us, removes our sin even as we say yes to Him through the Spirit of God who draws us.

Forgiving us, He has made us holy and perfect in His sight. Holy = perfect. It means we are cleansed, forgiven, and made "right" with God. In speaking of "perfect" people, Paul is not talking about our performance but about our lack of guilt, something that comes about when we say "yes" to Jesus. When we accept His forgiveness, His blood washes us clean of the guilt we would otherwise carry and makes us righteous in His eyes. It's completely that simple. It has to do with those who, despite every stumbling, turn their eyes to Him and say again, "YES, Lord!"

"Yes, Lord. I failed. Yes, Lord. I need You. Yes, Lord. I give You my sin. Yes, Lord. I accept Your forgiveness and receive Your cleansing. Yes, Lord. I thank You for restoring me! Yes, Lord. Because of Your mercy I stand perfect before You, clean, and free from guilt!"

As often as it is necessary, we continue to place our trust in Him. As a parent changes her baby's diaper again and again and again, because the baby continues to need it again and again and again, God continues to forgive us again and again and again, because we need it again and again and again. Having committed Himself to clean up after us as often as necessary, all He asks is that we be ready to call to Him for help and forgiveness when we need it.

Hudson Taylor, the missionary who founded the China Inland Mission in the mid-1800s, said, "The Lord Jesus received is holiness begun. The Lord Jesus cherished is holiness advancing. The Lord Jesus counted upon as never absent is holiness complete. He is most holy who has most of Christ within..."1

In short, holiness is more who we know than what we do.

Paul says it this way:

> *"More than that, I count all things to be loss in view of the surpassing value of knowing Christ Jesus my Lord, for whom I have suffered the loss of all things, and count them but rubbish*

Philippians 3:8-9

Made righteous through the gift of His forgiveness, God frees us,
restoring us to perfection in His eyes like a baby freshly changed
out of a dirty diaper – washed and fresh in his mother's arms. In
that place there is joy and freedom! We are called to live in this new
lifestyle of being restored and "perfect."

Have the attitude of trust. Yearn to live in surrender to Him. Reject
the temptation to depend on your ability to perform for Him. Say
"yes" to Him regularly.

As a child longs to be in his mother's arms, Paul tells us that we who
have been made perfect by the forgiveness of Christ need to have
that same attitude. Longing to be in the Father's arms, we yearn to
remain in the life of surrender that He has made possible through
His Spirit. As He washes our sin away, we can experience more than
just moments of freedom from guilt. We will find a lifestyle shaped
by freedom and joy.

If your attitude is different than this...

If you cannot get past a sense of needing to perform for God...

If you just cannot seem to get over your sense of self-hatred for all of
the failures that have marked your life, God will show you the truth
about who you are in Christ, if you allow Him to do so. He will
convince you that you can let go and trust Him. "Let us therefore, as
many as are perfect, have this attitude; and if in anything you have
a different attitude, God will reveal that also to you" *(Philippians
3:15)*. Call on Him to do this and then let Him do it.

Knowing this, we are called to continue to live according to the
standard of holiness that we have obtained by faith in Christ. Don't
let go of living in the righteousness of Jesus. Don't let go of the goal
of a surrendered life. Our tendency is to wander back to the old way
of carrying our own guilt, especially since it is so logical to do so.
Trusting Jesus allows us to take heart. Isaiah speaks of this in calling

us to wait upon the Lord, allowing Him to renew our strength *(Isaiah 40:31)*.

Just as living in Christ doesn't depend on our strength, but on His, so living in Christ doesn't depend on our loving Him first. It depends on Him loving us first *(1 John 4:19)*.

Living in Christ doesn't depend on us keeping our noses clean. It depends on surrendering to the One who cleanses us with the blood of our Savior Jesus.

We just say "yes" to Him. Determinedly.

According to the Apostle John, *"The Son of God appeared for this purpose, to destroy the works of the devil"* *(1 John 3:8)*. Jesus, in shedding his blood, has destroyed the power of sin, death, and the devil. Those who live in the reality of His cleansing live already perfected in the sense that they live in His forgiveness and are protected by His righteousness. Against this righteousness, the accusations of the devil, accusations of guilt and failure, fall powerless and shattered for all eternity.

Hold to it! Live in it. Say "yes" to Him again and again. Determinedly!

Pray: Come, Holy Spirit. I give this time to You, in Jesus' name.

Pray: Dear Father, I accept Jesus' righteousness today by faith. I accept that His blood has washed my sins away and that I stand clean and protected by You. I renounce the lies and accusations of the devil. Strip his influence from my life and send him to where You send him, Jesus. As You cleanse me of my imperfections, I stand in Your perfection. I accept that I am righteous before You, because of the gift of Christ.

Lord, live through me. Even when there are consequences from my sin that I may have to live with in this world, let me live as though I believe I am actually guilt free. Let the love and joy that Jesus demonstrated while He was on earth be mine. I bless You for the gift You have given me in Him. In this moment, I surrender once more to Your grace and forgiveness. I give You every wandering thought and deed. I accept my life in You, Lord, in Jesus' name. Amen.

Day 24

Join in Following My Example

"...however, let us keep living by that same standard to which we have attained.
Brethren, join in following my example, and observe those who walk according to the pattern you have in us."

Philippians 3:16-17

Each of us need mentors. These are the people we are going to imitate and be deliberate about learning life lessons from. It is one thing to sit in a Bible class and learn biblical knowledge, but it is often quite another thing to apply that knowledge in everyday life. Mentors help us by giving us a model to imitate, helping us move from the classroom into an effective daily life in Christ. The coaching we get from a live mentor is invaluable. The first disciples got this kind of coaching directly from Jesus Himself.

Jesus mentored in a radical way. Walking the shores of the Sea of Galilee, He called His first disciples. Leaving their nets and their family businesses, they followed Jesus into the unknown. They didn't just go with Him on a nine-to-five basis, but actually went and lived with Him. As they walked with Jesus and absorbed His teachings, they watched Him put His teachings into action, awestruck at what they experienced. When Jesus felt they had learned enough and were ready for more, He sent them out to do ministry in teams of two. With only each other to consult, and Jesus' model of ministry to imitate, they began to do ministry as He did. The results were powerful!

Though we will never find a human mentor as qualified as Jesus, there are many mentors out there with much to give. As I think back on the mentors in my life, most of them did not come looking for me. I had to learn how to find them for myself.

Searching for a mentor is a deliberate endeavor that requires an understanding of what you want as well as some knowledge of what a healthy mentor looks like. Pray for God's leading and begin to observe the people of faith who live around you. You are looking for someone who lives a life marked with faith, love, hope, and freedom – evidence of a life lived by the guidance and power of the Holy Spirit *(Galatians 5:22-23; 1 Corinthians 13:13).*

Once you have found someone who lives in obvious dependence on God, ask that person if you can meet together to discuss life and what it means to follow Jesus. If they agree to your request, begin to spend time with them. Ask them to share with you where they got the faith to live as they do. Listen to their life story. Join them in their devotional disciplines. Ask them if you can help them as they go to serve God in the places God has given them to do so. Don't expect your mentor to be perfect in the way they live their faith. Only Jesus was perfect in that way. Watch how they handle themselves when they stumble, as well as when they experience victories. Apply what you see to your own life.

As we live and walk with such people, their lifestyle begins to rub off on us. What we have come to know conceptually begins to find its way into both our living and our relationships. What we could not easily bring to application on our own comes more naturally as we walk with someone who is so familiar with trusting God that their life is built around living that way. As we watch them trust God for things that we would normally have taken into our own hands to make happen, we get to see God honor their trust with His provision. Search out someone who has made it a practice to live beyond their abilities in that place of faith where only God can be the support that they need.

Look for someone who lives after the pattern of the apostles and whose lifestyle is a faith-based one, marked by trust and surrender to the Holy Spirit. The need to possess things is not the main priority in the life of a Christ-like mentor. Their priorities are in line with Jesus' priorities, rather than being defined by the world. Seeking to live in the presence of God above all else, they are motivated as Jesus was, to see the lost saved and believers equipped for service in line with the great commission of *Matthew 28:19 – "Go therefore and make disciples of all the nations..."*

It can be difficult to find someone like the person I have described. You might be the only follower of Christ that you know of in your context. If so, be encouraged. Even though Jesus no longer physically walks the earth, He has sent His Holy Spirit to those who believe and has promised never to leave you alone. Be open to the work of the Holy Spirit and get a good study Bible. Using the Bible, His Spirit will teach you. Build regular time with Him into your life as you would build in time with any other mentor. Take your Bible in hand. Begin your reading in the gospels and read the New Testament through. Study the stories of Jesus. Observe how he related to His Heavenly Father and to those around Him. Study the teachings of the apostles in the epistles, watchful for how they might lead you closer to Jesus.

It can be helpful to see the Bible as being made up of categories called "teachings" and "stories." The teaching sections are the parts where instruction is given. The stories describe situations in the lives of Jesus, His apostles, and others. While the teaching parts contain the truths we need to know about God and about who we are in Christ, the stories show us how Jesus and His apostles applied those truths to everyday life and ministry. As you read the teachings, ask the Holy Spirit to embed those truths in your life. As you read the stories, ask Christ to show you how He and His apostles ministered and imitate them. The things of God will begin to happen around you as you do so, because of the faith you have begun to live and walk in. The day will come when God gathers others around you to share and have relationships with as you grow in serving Him. In all likelihood, and if you are willing, you will soon become a mentor yourself.

Pray: Come, Holy Spirit. I give this time to You, in Jesus' name.

Pray: Spirit of God, I need mentors. I need someone in whom I can see Your grace working. I need someone whose example will encourage me on to greater trust in You. Show me those who follow You and bring me into a relationship that can help me grow. Lord, I want to follow Paul's example. I want to walk in that place of surrender and faith that He speaks of. Open Your Word to me. Show me Your teachings. Lead me in applying Your Word to my daily life.

Lord, forgive me for the times when I have read Your Word and looked at the lifestyle of the New Testament believers, unable to believe that I could live in the way they did. In those moments, I pulled back from those biblical believers whose example could have taught me. Forgive me for the times when I believed that following You, like your disciples did, couldn't be done today. I renounce this lie and I accept that living for You, as they did, is possible even today. Just as You provided for Your disciples back then, I accept Your promise to provide for me today. Lead me in stepping out. Lead me in increasing my trust in You. I want to see Your presence and Your power working in and through me just like Your early disciples experienced it. Thank You for answering my prayer, in Jesus' name. Amen.

Day 25

Many Walk as Enemies

"...however, let us keep living by that same standard to which we have attained. Brethren, join in following my example, and observe those who walk according to the pattern you have in us. For many walk, of whom I often told you, and now tell you even weeping, that they are enemies of the cross of Christ, whose end is destruction, whose god is their appetite, and whose glory is in their shame, who set their minds on earthly things."

Philippians 3:16-19

The cross of Christ stands for the death of selfishness. It stands for an end to a lifestyle in which we are supposedly in control and God's way is viewed as an infringement on our right to live the way we want. The cross calls us to surrender self-glorification so that we can point people to Christ.

Paul warns of a religious group that he calls "enemies of the cross of Christ." Not speaking about unbelievers in general, He is describing a part of our society made up of people who both know and understand who Jesus claimed to be, but who deliberately resist the message of the gospel because they see it as being dangerous to their lifestyle. Sometimes even identifying themselves as believers, other than possible church attendance, there is little evidence of a relationship with Jesus in their daily living. Paul wanted the followers of Christ to gain some understanding of how an enemy of the cross may act and live in order to guard against being influenced by them.

Living as an enemy means choosing to live in a manner that is deliberately hostile to what Jesus stood for. Paul tells us that many people in New Testament times lived as enemies of Christ. The same is true today.

Though enemies of the cross may exhibit a number of qualities, Paul speaks of those who live a punishing lifestyle; punishing of self and punishing of others. Holding up their lives as billboards for all to see what they have "done" for God, according to Paul their identity is in their shame rather than in the freedom Jesus grants those who serve Him. Their focus of living is all about themselves and their accomplishments. It's not about Jesus.

Enemies of the cross demonstrate, by the way that they live, that a lifestyle of surrender to the living God is not a priority for them. Not understanding the freedom of being able to abandon themselves to His care, their lives are marked with fear, greed, and manipulation as they live, day in and day out, trying to make their lives work the way they want them to. If they pray at all, their prayer is, "Please, God, give me the life that I want!"

An enemy of the cross is someone who is determined to have their way rather than God's way. An enemy of the cross may seek an end to the pain while hanging onto the lifestyle that is causing the pain. As an enemy of the cross, I can love my sin and still say I want to follow God when, in fact, I really just want my sin to be blessed, so that I can maintain the appearance of being godly while pursuing my own agenda.

An enemy of the cross responds in fear every time he gets close to the cross, because at the cross Jesus Christ demands all that we are. It is a place of death – death to self-interests, to selfish appetites, and to all that has held our allegiance. It is a place of laying it all down. It means taking the risk to trust God with all that I am and have. Am I ready? Are you? Many are not. We can wear the Christian badge and still live a life of selfishness and self-service, but, if we choose the way of selfishness, our god is not the God who gave His all on the cross. With our selfishness preventing us from a relationship based on true worship of the Crucified Christ, we can lead no one to Him.

It's important to understand that Paul was not trying to be

condemnatory, nor was he devaluing these people. In spite of his strong language, he wept over them just like Jesus did over Jerusalem. Seeing the tragedy and knowing the end that awaits enemies of Christ and all who follow them, he also knew the danger they would pose to those who wanted to follow God's call.

Paul warns against following the example of an enemy of the cross. He says they will lead us to the god of the belly – a god that can also be called the god of consumption. Taking pride in the awful things they have done, they control their followers with the same shame and peer pressure that they are controlled by.

It is different for a person who says "yes, Lord." For this person the cross stands for the death of Jesus, the death of Satan's power, the death of sin's grip on humanity, and the death of our old identity as enemies of God. Standing for the end of the separation that once existed between God and His people, the cross of Christ spells the end of condemnation. On the cross, Christ brought a horrible reality to an end in order that something new might be raised up in its place.

The cross brought an end to despair in order that hope could be born again in the human heart. The cross shattered the unrealistic and worldly expectations of a whole people worldwide and opened the way for a heavenly perspective on life. The cross brought an end to Satan's control, to the illusion of human control, to the world being out of control. The cross turned existing into living, making it possible for us to thrive rather than just survive.

Jesus calls us to something greater than this world can give us, but we have to understand that the road to our calling is through the cross. Called to embrace Him in His death, so that we may live with Him in His life, that choice will cost us everything.

So what are we afraid of? Are you like me – afraid of losing everything you have in your hands right now for the sake of a promise that you have only heard and read about? Are you afraid to admit that you are too in love with your right to have life as you want it to let go of it easily?

Yet, like me, you hear His voice.

We sense His calling as He draws us forward to the cross. I have decided that I am ready to say "yes" to Him. Are you ready?

Pray: Come, Holy Spirit. I give this time to you, in Jesus' name.

Pray: Lord, I want it to be true. All that You say about me living in You and You living in me. I want it to be true in my life. I confess that I have been addicted to this world. I have not lived for You. I have lived for myself. I confess that I have sought Your blessing for what I wanted in this life rather than really giving my life to You. Jesus, like the Apostle Paul spoke in Romans 7:14-25, I know and I experience a battle that goes on within me. My "self" battles for control in that place, and the devil hinders me from complete surrender to You.

Lord, I now understand that the cross is about dying to who I used to be and what I used to hang onto. Jesus, I come to the cross and I offer You what has kept me from living as one of your own.

(What are those things that you have feared you would lose if you really offered your life to serve Jesus? List them on a paper.)

I confess and renounce my idolatry over these things, Jesus. I give each of them to You at the cross. I place them under Your blood and I renounce their control over my life. I say "yes" to You in the places where my idols have held me. Jesus, I accept Your forgiveness. I accept your calling to die to this old selfish way of living. I accept my freedom in You and the new life to which You call me.

I want to cherish the cross, to live in what You did there, and to know the freedom that only comes as I die to one world in order to live in the next. Only You can strip me of all other gods. Protect me from worshipping the gods of appetite for the things of this world. In Jesus' name, I ask this. Amen.

Day 26

He Will Transform our Humble State

"For our citizenship is in heaven, from which also we eagerly wait for a Savior, the Lord Jesus Christ; who will transform the body of our humble state into conformity with the body of His glory, by the exertion of the power that He has even to subject all things to Himself."

Philippians 3:20-21

I do not belong to this world.

It's a good thing to be reminded of. In a number of Paul's writings we are told that, once we give our lives to Christ, we no longer belong to this world. We belong to heaven. Jesus taught His disciples that, because they no longer belonged to this world, they could expect poor treatment from the world while they were here. Having accepted the call to follow Him, their citizenship changed their identity. They didn't fit here anymore.

 With the change in citizenship, came a new set of rights. Citizens of heaven view their "rights" differently than citizens of the world. This world's rights are self-centered, geared to protecting our "self." Heaven's rights are un-self-centered and are geared to living fully as we were originally created to live. When we surrendered to the call of God and gave our lives to Christ, we exchanged our citizenship in this world and the rights that go with it for our citizenship in heaven and the "rights" that come with belonging to the family of God.

 Due to the fact that there is no condemnation for those who are in

Christ, followers of Jesus have the right to insist on the forgiveness that is ours rather than having to pay for our own sins *(Romans 8:1)*. We have the right to expect that God's joy will be our strength in trying circumstances. We have the right to know that God is using us to touch this world with hope. We have the right to never be alone because He promises to be with us always. When the devil attacks us, we have the right to stand in Christ's authority and command the enemy to flee. As we live hidden in Christ rather than becoming another of the enemy's victims, we have the right to the fruit that Jesus brings to a life lived in the power of His Spirit *(Galatians 5:22-23)*.

Ultimately, we have the right to anticipate eternity with God.

Knowing that we have been made for eternity, and that Jesus has prepared a place in heaven for us, causes us to anticipate going home to be with Him. Like a traveler who gets tired of living out of suitcases and in motels, a time comes when we are ready to settle into a place where we belong. Every believer yearns for more than what this world offers, because, once we say "yes" to Jesus, we can never be fully satisfied with life here on earth again.

Are you one of those people who said "yes" to Jesus and noticed that the challenges of life did not suddenly disappear? Do you live with the sense that something is still missing? Are you still yearning for more? Paul says that the yearning for something that is missing is normal. Our lives cannot be totally fulfilled this side of heaven, because we belong to eternity and, knowing that, we wait eagerly for the time when that promise becomes reality.

We wait for Jesus' return.

Jesus told His disciples that He was going to prepare a place for them and that He would also come back to get them *(John 14:2)*. Paul tells us that the day is coming when we will see Christ come again. The sky will be rolled back and he will appear to us in the clouds. In that moment, we will be caught up from this earth and we will meet Him in the air. We will be changed and every flaw will be removed as our old earthly body is transformed into a heavenly body. This will happen to all who are followers of Jesus, even to those who died believing in Christ. The decay of the grave will be replaced with vibrant, living, heavenly flesh as we are lifted from the earth at the call of the returning Savior. All imperfection will be done away with as God brings full restoration to His creation *(1 Corinthians 15:51-52; 1 Thessalonians 4:15-17)*.

According to *John 1:1-3*, the power of Christ created all that has been created, including the universe and the earth around us. We look forward to full restoration on that day when Jesus will "exert" in us His full power – a power that raised Him from the dead, healed the sick, and cast out demons
(Phil 3:21). Exerting His power in each of us who have simply said "yes" to Him, the Spirit of Jesus will work this restoration in us and we will become as He is. This is what we look forward to. This is our right as believers.

This is such a vitally important point that I want to say it again. We will not just be raised spiritually, as though we were ghosts. We will be raised with our physical bodies transformed as He demonstrates His power to redeem all that was lost. When Jesus appeared to His disciples after His resurrection, He made it clear to them that they were looking at more than a ghost by inviting them to touch His wounds in order to prove that He had been physically raised from the dead. Paul says that Jesus will "conform" us to Him. He will make us like He became after His resurrection, with our whole self fully remade. In doing so, God intends to demonstrate total victory over all forms of death and decay, including physical death itself. We, as those who are made in the image of God – body, soul, and spirit *(1 Thessalonians 5:23)* – will be fully restored in Christ for all eternity.

I am looking forward to that day. I do yearn for more. I do not fit this world. My citizenship is in heaven and I look forward to celebrating Christ's return with anticipation.

Pray: Come, Holy Spirit. I give this time to You, in Jesus' name.

Pray: Lord Jesus, I accept my identity in You, and claim my rights as a citizen of heaven. I invite You to transform me, to fill me with hope. I renounce my own performing and striving to make this life work, as though my citizenship was of this earth. Wherever I have lived as though I still belong to this world, forgive me. I give myself fully to You. I am Yours, Lord Jesus, in Your holy name. Amen!

Day 27

Help These Women

"Therefore, my brothers, you whom I love and long for, my joy and crown, that is how you should stand firm in the Lord, dear friends! I plead with Euodia and I plead with Syntyche to be of the same mind in the Lord. Yes, and I ask you, my true companion, help these women since they have contended at my side in the cause of the Gospel, along with Clement and the rest of my co-workers, whose names are in the book of life."

Philippians 4:1-3 (NIV)

"Therefore..."

"Therefore" means "as a result of."

As a result of knowing what Paul has said up to this point, we are called to action. Called by Christ to live in surrender to the Spirit of God, those of us who have said "yes" to a relationship with Jesus have our identity with Him in heaven. Considering ourselves to be strangers in this world, we understand that we don't really fit here and live in anticipation of an eternity with Jesus.

"My brothers, you whom I love and long for, my joy and crown, that is how you should stand firm in the Lord, dear friends!"

The Apostle speaks as though we, who believe in Christ, are a family. As brothers and sisters, we are not alone. When we say "yes" to Christ, *1 Corinthians 12:24-26* tells us that the Spirit of God joins us to the family of God in such intimacy that, when one of us hurts, all the rest of the family are impacted by our pain as well. When one of us is joyous, all the rest are touched by our joy.

In the family of God, the things that impact us individually, to some extent, impact all of us. It's a very different concept than the one that many of us grew up with. Often we have been taught to look after our own interests first and to distance ourselves from those whom we don't like, or who don't serve our purposes, while attaching ourselves to those who have something to offer us. Christ taught the opposite. He said we are to give to those who cannot give in return and to love those who don't love us back. Jesus' disciples came from diverse backgrounds and would not normally have hung out together. Their connection with each other was centered on Him, just as ours is today. As a part of the global family of believers, our connection with each other goes deeper than the world's way of connecting. We belong and can never be truly alone, regardless of disagreements and personality clashes.

That said, often the Christian Church falls short of the ideal Jesus taught.

The relationships that develop between those who have shared in ministry are often deeper than any others. Along with that depth comes an increased ability to hurt one another. It was the same in Paul's day, just as it is now, and we find him working to heal a rift between two people who had been partners in ministry together. Pleading with two believing Christians to look deeper than their anger, he asks them to remember their common identity in Christ.

> *"I plead with Euodia and I plead with Syntyche to be of the same mind in the Lord."*

I could hear Paul saying something like this: "People, remember that you are brothers and sisters in Christ! Whatever is dividing you, look deeper than the situation, forgive each other and get past it." Reminding them of what once united them, he emphasized their common bond in Christ and asked them to work out the issue that was between them, to lay down their pride, anger, and the offense they had taken against each other, to forgive and be forgiven.

Called to remember what unites us as believers, unity in the relationships we have with God and each other is foundational to the strength of our Christian communities. Knowing that, Satan's attack is always aimed at destroying the unity among us. The devil knows that if he can do this, he can also destroy the witness and ministry we have in our communities.

In the Garden of Eden, Satan succeeded in destroying the relationships God created us for. Convincing Eve and Adam that they did not need God and that they could be like God with the ability to live their lives by their own resources, he succeeded in separating them from God. Having lost their relationship with God, they turned on one another, even accusing God Himself of being partially responsible for their sin. Every society since that time has struggled with division. God sought to reverse what happened in the garden by creating a worldwide family, centered in Christ, where the love of God and unity of the Holy Spirit can restore relationships destroyed by selfishness and division.

Satan always attacks us in our unity in Christ and our love for one another. Fostering disagreements on issues such as doctrine, parenting philosophies, or worship styles, the enemy seeks to get us fighting one another for control. Division in the Church happens as we become willing to take offense against each other. Using whatever he can, the devil strives to separate us from each other.

Wherever Satan can introduce conflict, he makes pride the main issue, destroying the witness of God's people and the intimacy of the community of faith.

For the sake of the whole community, Paul asked these two leading women to come together. In asking them to look deeper than their immediate issue with each other, he challenged them to lay aside whatever separated them and to find unity in their worship of Christ. Directing them to their common belief in the person of the resurrected Jesus, he asked them to remember the great command of Jesus to love each other as they loved themselves *(Matthew 22:37-39).*

> *"Yes, and I ask you, my true companion, help these women since they have contended at my side in the cause of the Gospel, along with Clement and the rest of my co-workers, whose names are*

in the book of life."

Paul knew what betrayal and offense felt like. He knew how difficult it was to let go of hurts and to make amends with someone you no longer liked. Encouraging the other believers not to leave these two alone in their struggle to reconcile, he called the Church to gather around them and to help them. Paul asked the Church to pray for them without gossiping about their issues, to support them without trying to pretend that nothing had happened, and to encourage each of them to see the other's value without succumbing to the temptation to take sides.

A friend of mine once spoke about how his community in Africa would draw together around couples who were having relational problems. He described a community that got involved when a marriage was facing breakdown in order to help bring reconciliation. Support was given to the man by the men and to the woman by the women. Refusing to leave the couple on their own to decide whether or not they would work it out, no one "respected their privacy." Everyone got involved. The Church community was deliberate in coming around those in need to provide strength and encouragement.

As a part of being in the family of God together, we are called to help each other come together in the unity that we have in Christ. Standing undivided, we become the presence of God on this earth together.

Pray: Lord, draw Your Church together around those in the body of Christ who are divided. Protect us from seeing things through the perspective of offenses given or received. Protect us from taking sides. Protect us from valuing one above another.

Lord, I want to be as Your presence in Your body. I accept my calling to love and to be loved. I give You my immaturity and accept Your forgiveness for the times when I have pulled back from those who needed me, because I was too embarrassed or shy to show my love and support. Jesus, I am Yours. Live through me. Defeat the selfish and dividing work of the devil among us. Make me an effective and real witness of Your love. In Jesus' mighty name, I pray. Amen.

Day 28

Stand

"Finally, be strong in the Lord and in his mighty power. Put on the full armor of God so that you can take your stand against the devil's schemes. For our struggle is not against flesh and blood, but against the rulers, against the authorities, against the powers of this dark world and against the spiritual forces of evil in the heavenly realms. Therefore put on the full armor of God, so that when the day of evil comes, you may be able to stand your ground, and after you have done everything, to stand. Stand firm then, with the belt of truth buckled around your waist, with the breastplate of righteousness in place, and with your feet fitted with the readiness that comes from the Gospel of peace. In addition to all this, take up the shield of faith, with which you can extinguish all the flaming arrows of the evil one. Take the helmet of salvation and the sword of the Spirit, which is the word of God."

Ephesians 6:10-17 (NIV)

Paul places our world and our flesh into a spiritual context, indicating that the struggles we face in living out our Christian lives are not always as they seem. In verse 12, he clearly states that our battle is not against flesh and blood but against "spiritual forces."

As we come to understand that there is a spiritual root to the problems we face, we can then deal with the core of our struggle from a biblical perspective. A fourfold repetition of the call to "stand", in the passage above, makes it clear that we have a part to play in actively resisting demonic spiritual forces as a part of our walk with Christ.

The Apostle Peter agrees with Paul when he states in 1 Peter 5:8 that everyone who follows Christ experiences spiritual attack on a regular basis. Peter is speaking to believers when he says that our enemy, the devil, prowls around like a roaring lion seeking those whom he might devour. This illustration describes ongoing action by a predatory enemy against believers who have a tendency to be unaware of the dangers lurking nearby. Warned to be aware, we remain standing in Christ and safe from the predator, refusing to give the enemy the opportunity that he seeks.

The teaching of Peter and Paul presupposes that it is actually possible for the devil to attack us effectively and that there can be a danger of us falling to his attack. To that end, Paul speaks of our spiritual armor.

It was morning. I was doing my devotional reading on *Ephesians 6:10-17* and praying on the armor when I was stopped by a sense that God's Spirit was speaking to me. Asking me to stop viewing the armor simply as items of hardware that I wore spiritually, I was to look up associated scriptures that spoke of what the armor of God really represented. I was amazed to discover that the armor actually represented Jesus Christ Himself. As I read, it struck me that to put the armor on meant to clothe myself in Christ.

It changed the way I saw the call to "stand."

When Paul called believers to stand, he meant they were to take their stand "in" Christ – not just on His behalf. This new understanding made taking my "stand" more about His grace and power surrounding and empowering me and less about my own determination to be strong.

In being clothed with the Armor of God, Paul says:

We are to be belted up with the truth. In *John 14:6*, Jesus calls Himself the Truth.

We are to put on righteousness as a breastplate. *Romans 3:21-22* says that Jesus' own righteousness is ours and is received by faith.

We are to take our stand in the shoes of the Gospel of peace. *Colossians 1:20* says that Jesus made peace for us by the blood of the cross. Secure footing brings an element of peace to every challenge that we face knowing that, whatever the struggle, we stand in what Jesus accomplished on the cross.

We are to put on the salvation of Christ as our helmet, literally meaning to be saved, or delivered, from our old thought-life. *Romans 12:1-2* goes on to elaborate by saying that we are to be transformed by the renewing of our minds. If we are to give ourselves more deeply to Christ, our old perspectives and guiding philosophies of life must undergo radical change. We literally need to be set free from the old ways of thinking that have guided us through our lives up to this point.

We are to take up the shield of faith. The Apostle Peter says that we are "protected (shielded) by the power of God through faith" *(1 Peter 1:5)*. We carry the protection of God with us wherever we go as we actively, and continuously, entrust ourselves to God's hand moment by moment and situation by situation, despite the attacks of the enemy.

We are given the sword of the Spirit, the Word of God, made living and active by the Holy Spirit as described in *Hebrews 4:12-16*. As it exposes and discerns thoughts and intents of the heart, God uses His Word to bring us to conviction and repentance. Destroying the lies and cutting through the deceit in our lives where the enemy does his greatest work as he seeks to destroy us, God's Word lays our hearts bare in the presence of God, so that we can receive the forgiveness He offers.

Paul makes it clear that we need to actively stand in these biblical realities on an ongoing basis. Unable to depend on ourselves to accomplish victory, in "standing" we depend on the finished work of Christ alone. These pieces of armor actually refer to Jesus Himself. Living "in" Christ is a reality that every believer needs to appropriate daily. *Romans 13:14* tells us to "put on the Lord Jesus Christ..." As we put on the armor through prayer, we find ourselves wrapped in His presence. His presence, like armor, protects us from spiritual attack.

So what happens to those who succumb to temptation, step out from their dependence on Christ, and do give the enemy an opportunity? The Apostle John tells us to give our failings to Jesus right away and He will take care of them. He says that "if anyone (of us) sins, we have an Advocate with the Father, Jesus Christ..." Our advocate, or "one who speaks on our behalf," is Jesus Himself. In the moment of our confession, He is faithful and just and cleanses us from all unrighteousness *(1 John 1:9 – 2:1)*.

It is good to be reminded regularly that, as we put on the armor, we are really putting on Christ Himself. To stand in the armor means to stand in Christ. As we stand in Christ, we are safe. When we try to live by our own strength, in the way Adam and Eve chose to do, we become vulnerable. Continue standing in Jesus! When we "pray the armor on," know that we are really putting on the presence of Jesus, Himself.

Pray: Come, Holy Spirit. I give this time to you.

Pray: Heavenly Father, I hide myself in Christ so that it is no longer I who live, but Christ who lives in me (Galatians 2:20).

I now accept the truth of Christ as my belt of truth. I declare that no deceit of the enemy has power over me. As Jesus is the truth, and His Spirit leads me into truth, I accept the freedom that His truth brings.

I accept the righteousness of Christ as my heart's covering. I can no longer be effectively accused of guilt by the enemy, because Jesus has made me clean by His blood.

I accept the Gospel of peace as my shoes. I take my stand in the cross, because *Colossians 1:20* states that God made me to be at peace with Him through Jesus' death on the cross. This peace prepares me for whatever lies ahead. I accept His peace. By the grace of God, I cannot be moved.

I accept the helmet of salvation. Lord Jesus, I give all of my thoughts to you. I command every thought of the enemy to be thrown down from my mind
(2 Corinthians 10:4-5). I renounce all old ways of thinking that are not in line with God's truth and I invite Jesus into every thought that I have. I accept the "mind of Christ" as my own *(1 Corinthians 2:16)*.

I accept the shield of faith. I do not depend on my own strength but on the power of Christ and His blood that covers me. Your word says that through faith I am shielded by the power of God. I accept and declare that every attack of the enemy is destroyed as it comes against God's power, which covers and shields me.

I accept the sword of the Spirit which is God's Word. It penetrates every darkness and exposes every deception. By the power of the Holy Spirit, it is living and active and it exposes everything before God in order that everything which is not of God might be rendered powerless. It lays everything bare and brings everyone accountable to God. By it, every power of Satan is thwarted.

Jesus, I stand in YOU. Amen.

Day 29

I Will Say It Again – Rejoice!

"Rejoice in the Lord always. I will say it again: Rejoice!"
Philippians 4:4 (NIV)

When this kind of repetition is used in the Bible, it means that the author is placing strong emphasis on something.

"Rejoice in the Lord always. Again I will say it: rejoice!" Strong emphasis is often used when someone or something is distracting us from where our focus needs to be.

There is so much that distracts: things we have to do, places we have to be, people we have to talk to, what to do with our money, what to do when we run short of money, working for the sake of getting more money, failed relationships, successful relationships, play time, work time, the need to make better use of our time, trauma, loss, anger, self-condemnation and the condemnation of others. On and on it goes.

What if we could actually live our lives as if God were in control?

What if we could be sure that God had us in His hand during times of loss, grief, loneliness, and failure? What about when we have to face the reality that life has not turned out the way we had imagined that it would? How about when we are faced with the aftermath of our own mistakes and have to live with those consequences? What about when we have been faced with the impact of someone else's mistakes while feeling helpless to do anything about how it has affected us? What about situations when everything within us is screaming that we don't know what we are doing?

Paul calls us to rejoice!

If anyone lived in a hostile, out of control, challenging environment, it was the early Christians. Called to worship one God in a society that prized the worship of many gods, their choice to follow Christ alone made them less than favored among their neighbors. The target of hostilities, the butt of prejudice in their business communities and in the rest of the culture of the day, persecuted and betrayed, life was not easy for these believers. Often in over their heads, they rarely had what could be called "security" from a worldly perspective.

A friend of mine, who gave his life to Jesus some years ago, experienced some of this kind of hardship as he gave up the worship of another god in favor of following Christ. A youth elder in the local congregation of a well-known cult, his day job was in the construction industry.

One day, on the jobsite where he worked, they hired a new guy fresh out of jail. It turned out that the New Guy had surrendered his life to Jesus while in prison. Having chosen my friend to share his story of salvation with, he shared it regularly. The New Guy's message was not polished, nor was it deep. In fact, it was pretty simple. Over and over the New Guy told my friend that, regardless of his arguments to the contrary, he was lost and going to hell unless he knew Jesus.

Having been well trained in the arguments of his religion, it turned out that, when faced with the New Guy's calm assertions, my friend found that he had no real confidence that any of his belief system was true. He had no peace. The New Guy had peace. Rejoicing in the Lord? He saw a freedom to do so in the New Guy that he did not have himself. The New Guy spoke of God's presence as being with him daily, but my friend had no sense of God's presence or any real confidence of God's protection over his life or his eternity. He felt alone.

In the face of the New Guy's oft-repeated statement, all of my friend's well-trained arguments began to crumble. After a couple of weeks, he finally couldn't take any more and asked this follower of Jesus what he had to do to get right with Christ. The New Guy became my friend's first brother-in-Christ as he surrendered to Jesus right there on the jobsite. Renouncing his old belief system, my friend entered a relationship with Christ. Overjoyed with the new peace he was experiencing, he also anticipated rough waters ahead, knowing that when he went home and told his folks there would be consequences for his decision.

His family argued with him. They tried to appeal to him. They threatened him. When that didn't work, they disowned him. They buried some of his clothing in the yard and told him that, as far as they were concerned, he was dead. Following that, his whole community rejected him and he found himself alone.

My friend later described his decision to follow Christ this way: "I didn't just give up a belief. I gave up my whole lifestyle to follow Jesus."

In the midst of all of the loss and struggle that came with his choice to follow Jesus, my friend entered his new life with a sense of amazement at how God was taking care of him. In the place of loss and rejection, Jesus was there, along with the New Guy and some other new brothers and sisters in Christ that he had just met. In a time when he had lost his family and many of his past relationships, he gained a sense of God being at his side and of the Spirit of Christ providing for him and leading him day by day. In speaking to him, I found myself inspired. Having thought he would be depressed over his many losses, I saw a man who rejoiced and did so deliberately. In the midst of a time in his life where his difficulties could have easily distracted him from his new-found relationship with Christ, he found himself worshipping God and aware that he was not alone – knowing that the Spirit of Christ was leading him, preparing his way, and providing for him as he walked deeper and deeper into a life of serving Jesus.

Like my friend, we are called to a deliberate lifestyle of rejoicing in the Lord. Regardless of what happens to us, of the mistakes we make, of what we feel or do not feel, there is no place where we can go to escape the love of our God. The psalmist tells us that, even if we make our bed in the deepest sea or on the heights of the mountains, God is there *(Psalm 139:7-10)*. To follow Christ means challenges will come and that, as we learn to rejoice through those challenges, we will learn what trust means. In that process, the relationship with God as GOD will become real to us. Going where He leads us may mean that we end up leaving behind some of our valued relationships as some of our friends and family, who do not appreciate our commitment to Christ, pull away from us.

Christ has promised that He will never leave us alone. Calling us to place more than our eternity in his hands, He asks for our lives as well. Living with His praise on our lips, we can know that He is with us, guiding us, protecting us, and using us – even in our mistakes and even in seemingly overwhelming circumstances.

He never condemns us *(Romans 8:1)*. He comes to save us *(John 3:16-17)*. He always forgives us *(1 John 1:9)*. He gives strength to the weary and lifts up those who have utterly fallen *(Isaiah 40:28-31)*.

Knowing all of this, I will rejoice in the situation in which I find myself – amidst failures and disappointments, as well as in the successes. I will rejoice because, regardless of what the situation brings me, I know who has me in His hand in the midst of the situation. To rejoice in such times and places is to trust and to believe. It is an act of faith and, though it often takes a while for the feelings to catch up, Jesus has assured us that we are in the Father's hand and nothing will take us from His grasp *(John 10:28-29)*. Through every challenge and every failure, through every moment of being in over our heads, if we have said "yes" to His call on our life, then we belong to Him. He cannot fail us even if we fail Him.

Pray: Lord Jesus, I rejoice in You. I take this moment to rejoice in You. I give myself, and the situation(s) I am in right now, to You:

______________________________ (Name the situation/situations)

Forgive me for becoming distracted and losing my focus on You and Your Lordship in this place of my life. I renounce every tendency I have to handle my life situations on my own. I surrender to You once again and I rejoice. I bless You. I know that You are with me, because You say You are. I accept that You will never leave me or forsake me *(Hebrews 13:5)*. I know that I am in Your hands and nothing can take me from You. I now accept the power of Your Spirit poured into this day, this moment, and this situation. By the power of Your Spirit, I ask You to fill my heart with rejoicing. I am Yours. In Jesus' name, I praise You. Amen.

Day 30

The Lord is Near

"Rejoice in the Lord always; again I will say, rejoice! Let your gentle spirit be known to all men. The Lord is near."
Philippians 4:4-5

We can tell that the Lord is near by the peace and the ability to be at rest in the midst of challenging circumstances that He gives us. Jesus said:

"Come to Me, all who are weary and heavy-laden, and I will give you rest. Take My yoke upon you and learn from Me, for I am gentle and humble in heart, and you will find rest for your souls. For My yoke is easy and My burden is light."
Matthew 11:28-30

Jesus came to bring peace and rest into the lives of those of us who need it and haven't been able to find it. He came for those whose lives have made them into weary people. He came for the broken people, the run-down people. He came for those too depressed to get up in the morning because they've lost their hope.

One of the last things Jesus told His disciples was to wait on Him for something that He would send them, the promise of the Holy Spirit who was soon to be poured out into their lives *(Luke 24:49)*.

Living through His followers, His Spirit is a Spirit of power and gentleness as He reaches into the lives of those whom He loves. Gentle even when He is exposing the sin in our lives that holds us back from walking with Him, He never comes stomping through our lives harshly or callously. Filled with compassion, He comes with a gentle boldness tinged by an amazing grace.

In this manner, the Spirit of Jesus Himself lives through those of us who have said "yes" to Him. In order to reach people, He picks and calls those of us who know what it means to live lives of lostness. He does that so that we will pass on the sense of comfort and compassion that we ourselves have received.

> *"Blessed be the God and Father of our Lord Jesus Christ, the Father of mercies and God of all comfort, who comforts us in all our affliction so that we will be able to comfort those who are in any affliction with the comfort with which we ourselves are comforted by God."*
>
> *2 Corinthians 1:3-4*

We are the kind of people that Jesus came for. We have each needed His comfort at various times in our lives. We have known grief. Many of us have known depression, lostness, and brokenness. We may have some understanding of what others go through because we have been there ourselves. For those of us who know what it really means to be saved, we know it because Jesus found us when we were lost and saved us. Because we know what it means to be helpless to save ourselves, we have a compassion for others who struggle that we otherwise could not have. We, who have experienced the gentle touch of Jesus, remember over and over that Jesus did not come to condemn the fallen.

He came to demonstrate His love in the lives of those who live with hate – even the self-hate that can often be the most difficult kind of hate to let go of.

He came to bring hope to those who see nothing good when they look at the future.

He came to bring a gentle touch to those whose way of living and surviving has trained them to be anything but gentle.

We can rejoice knowing that it is not up to us to fix people. Though we are called to share a message of Jesus and His gift of forgiveness and mercy, it is not even up to us to make them understand. We are simply called to let the Spirit of Jesus live through us to those who need His mercy.

To live this way, we need to be filled with the Holy Spirit whose work it is to manifest the gentleness of His presence in our lives.

Paul tells us in *Galatians 5:22-23* that, when we walk by the Spirit, our lives will radiate the Spirit's presence and the qualities that mark Him. Gentleness is one of those qualities *(Galatians 5:23)*. When we walk by the Spirit, we will be Jesus' presence in this world, in our communities, among our co-workers, our families, and our friends.

Even among our enemies and those who hate us.

And so we rejoice. We know whose we are. We know that Christ is near to us by the power of His Spirit. We know who holds our situation in the palm of His hand. We know that He loves our unsaved loved ones more than we ever could and that He is reaching out to draw them to Himself. We know that we will see the evidence of His Kingdom around us in the coming days as we follow His leading.

Jesus, I want to say "yes" to You! Come, Holy Spirit!

Pray aloud: Dear Jesus, today I choose to deliberately rejoice in You! I know who You are. You are the Son of my God. You lived and died for the sins of all humanity. On the cross, You broke the dividing wall between God and the human race. You cried out, "It is finished!" *(John 19:30)*. Because of that moment, my life is in Your hands.

Today, once again, I give You my life. I give You my day and every situation that I bring to this day or that will develop during this day.

Lord, I rejoice because I know that You have me and all of my situations in Your hand. I praise You because You are near me right now. I give myself to You in order that You might demonstrate Your gentleness through me TODAY. Lord Holy Spirit, as You lead me this day, let Jesus touch someone through me. Let the gentleness You give me be evident to someone who needs Your compassion. Lord, I want to be used by You to love someone as You loved me.

Even as I pray this, I accept the answer to my prayer, in Jesus' name. Amen.

Day 31

"Yes, Lord."

"So when they had finished breakfast, Jesus said to Simon Peter, 'Simon, son of John, do you love Me more than these?' He said to Him, 'Yes, Lord; You know that I love You.' He said to him, 'Tend My lambs.' He said to him again a second time, 'Simon, son of John, do you love Me?' He said to Him, 'Yes, Lord; You know that I love You.' He said to him, 'Shepherd My sheep.' He said to him the third time, 'Simon, son of John, do you love Me?' Peter was grieved because He said to him the third time, 'Do you love Me?' And he said to Him, 'Lord, You know all things; You know that I love You.' Jesus said to him, 'Tend My sheep. Truly, truly, I say to you, when you were younger, you used to gird yourself and walk wherever you wished; but when you grow old, you will stretch out your hands and someone else will gird you, and bring you where you do not wish to go.' Now this He said, signifying by what kind of death he would glorify God. And when He had spoken this, He said to him, 'Follow Me!'"

John 21:15-19

Often we make commitments to God that we fail to carry out. Peter was Jesus' best friend and yet, when put to the test, he denied his relationship to Jesus three times, the last time cursing to add emphasis. The story of Peter's denial is described in detail in *Matthew 26*. In the moment that he uttered his third and last denial of Jesus, *"Peter remembered the word which Jesus had said, 'Before a rooster crows, you will deny Me three times.' And he went out and wept bitterly"*

(Matthew 26:75).

In order to save his own skin, Peter publicly renounced his earlier declarations of love for his Savior. This from a disciple and friend who had recently told his Master that *"Even though all may fall away because of You, I will never fall away"* (Matthew 26:33).

So much for being able to follow through on his commitments.

After this experience, Jesus went to the cross. Three days later, He rose from the dead, showing Himself to many and demonstrating His complete victory over all forms of sin and death. Shortly after that, Jesus appeared on the lakeshore where Peter and some of His other disciples were fishing.

That's right. Peter had gone back to fishing. Having made his declaration to follow Jesus and then seen his inability to do so, he went back to the only lifestyle he knew – fishing. Convinced that he was a mistake and did not have what it took to be a servant of God, the only thing he could think to do was turn back to his old way of making a living.

Jesus called them to shore and made breakfast for them. Having eaten breakfast, Jesus turned to Peter suddenly, asking him in front of the others gathered around them, "Simon, son of John, do you love me, more than these?" Three times Peter spoke back his love: "Yes, Lord; You know I love You." Three times Jesus' response was to give Peter a task: "Feed my lambs."

Believing that he was finished as a servant of God, Peter had given up and abandoned his sense of calling. Jesus was not finished with him though. Jesus had a purpose for doing what He was doing. Having come to restore him, Jesus would now call Peter on a journey that was based on faith rather than immature zeal and a drive to perform.

Those who actively follow Jesus often go through what Peter went through. As we experience His love and forgiveness, we get excited to follow and serve Him. All too often, in our immaturity, we fail to realize that our own zeal and excitement are not going to be enough to carry us on the journey ahead. When Peter made his declaration that he would follow Jesus even if all the rest turned away, he proclaimed that his love for Jesus was enough to carry him. Jesus tried to tell him that he did not have the strength to carry that commitment through, but Peter refused to hear it. He would show Jesus!

He did show Jesus. He did just as Jesus predicted. When faced with the cost of following Jesus, his instinct for self-preservation took over and he renounced his Savior. Though he was called by Jesus, he demonstrated that he did not have the strength to follow that calling.

It was in this place of failure that Jesus came to ask His question of Peter, "Do you love Me?" Peter's response? "Yes, Lord; You know that I love You." As Jesus asked the question again and again, it opened the wound of Peter's betrayal. Hurt to be asked that question a third time, and with all pretense thrown aside, Peter stood before Jesus and brokenly proclaimed his love for his Lord as well as the knowledge that he was not strong enough to live that love out.

How many of us have found ourselves in that same place? We have made our declarations of love to someone and found ourselves lacking the strength and commitment to follow through on our promises. We have made our declaration of love and service to God Himself and found ourselves pulling back as we finally come to realize how difficult the journey is going to be. All of us have some of Peter in us.

Jesus knows this better than we do. He knew it when He called us. He may have warned us and we refused to listen, because we were sure that we knew better. In the end, we failed Him. Still in love with our Savior, but destroyed by our failure to live for Him, we did what Peter did. We went back to the only life we knew.

As He did with Peter, Jesus approaches us in our failure and asks, "Do you love Me?" He doesn't ask, "Can you live for Me?" He asks, "Do you love Me?" He doesn't want to know if we can do the job He has for us. He wants to know if we love Him.

Knowing Peter's inability and knowing that Peter now knew it as well, Jesus essentially said, "Good. Now that we have it straight that you can't live for Me by your own strength, My Spirit will become your strength and you will be My servant wherever I lead you. I am not interested in you living for Me. I am interested in living through you. There is a difference between those two approaches to following Me."

The promise of Jesus, in *Luke 24:49* and *Acts 1:8,* was that He would pour out His Spirit on His followers. We are not called to live for Jesus out of our own power and zeal. If we insist on doing so, we will fail. In learning this lesson, many of us will experience something like Peter did where we come to understand, in a deep way, that our strength is not enough to enable us to follow Jesus. Into that place of failure, Jesus comes to restore us. He comes to say, as he did to Peter, "You may be done with me, but I am not done with you! Do you love Me? It is enough. Give me what you have and come, follow Me!"

Jesus is the Redeemer. In that we rejoice. In that we have hope. In that our freedom lies. Whatever our failure, He can make it right. Empowering us by His Spirit, He comes to any place of weakness in which He can exercise His strength. Desiring to use us, He simply asks if we love Him, rather than if we love Him enough to make things happen for Him.

Do you love Him enough to give Him what you have? It can all be expressed in the simple response of Peter:

"Yes, Lord; You know that I love You."

Pray with me.

Prayer time: Take a minute and quiet your heart. Speak to Him, "Jesus, I am here. Come, Lord Holy Spirit."

Pray: Dear Lord Jesus, I praise You that You are my God. I praise You that You are to me as You were to Peter. I thank You that, even though I have shown my weaknesses over and over again, You have not abandoned me to the life I deserve. Jesus, I come to You to give You what I have. Forgive me for the times where I have insisted on trying to follow You in my own strength and zeal. Forgive me for the many times that I have acted as though I knew myself better than You know me. Lord, You see me as I am. Thank You that what You care about is my love for You. Please teach me how to love you, Lord.

(Take a moment of quiet and rest in His presence.)

Lord Jesus, I accept Your calling. I give you what I have. I wait on You for what You will do in me and the strength that You will give me as You take me forward on the journey to which You have called me. I receive and rejoice in Your forgiveness and mercy. Your kingdom come in my life and Your will be done in my life as it is in heaven. I say, "Yes, Lord." I am in Your hands, in Jesus' name. Amen.

Notes

1. *Hudson Taylor's Spiritual Secret*, Discovery House Pub., 1990. p. 175